IMAGES
of America

INDIANAPOLIS
SOCIAL CLUBS

The first public swimming pool in Indianapolis was located at the intersection of Delaware and South Streets in the early 1900s. The structure was not built as a pool but was the bottom section of a natural gas storage tank no longer used by the utility company. (Indiana Historical Society, Bass Photograph Collection No. 29676.)

On the cover: The members and their families celebrated the Fourth of July holiday weekend in 1925 at the pool of the Highland Golf and Country Club in this view from the front of the new clubhouse. A modern pool occupies the site today. (Highland Golf and Country Club.)

IMAGES
of America

INDIANAPOLIS
SOCIAL CLUBS

Jim Hillman and John Murphy

ARCADIA
PUBLISHING

Published by Arcadia Publishing
Charleston SC, Chicago IL, Portsmouth NH, San Francisco CA

Library of Congress Catalog Card Number: 2008935277

For all general information contact Arcadia Publishing at:
Telephone 843-853-2070
Fax 843-853-0044
E-mail sales@arcadiapublishing.com
For customer service and orders:
Toll-Free 1-888-313-2665

Visit us on the Internet at www.arcadiapublishing.com

*To Jim and Sandy Hillman and Jack and Agnes Murphy, the parents
who provided us with the memories, and to our children's children, so
that these times may never be forgotten*

CONTENTS

ACKNOWLEDGMENTS

As we began this book, we discovered that we had chosen a topic that interested many but for which there is precious little in the way of archived material. The Indianapolis-Marion County Public Library, the Indiana State Library, the Indiana Historical Society, and the Beech Grove Library each provided bits and pieces for which we are grateful.

However, it is the assistance of the managers and members of the clubs that still exist, and the former members of the ones now gone, that made this book possible. We can never express fully our thanks to the managers and members at the country clubs who literally took pictures off the walls to allow us to use them, the people who dug out family photo albums and allowed us access to their memories, and the people who gave us clues to locating long-lost newspaper archives.

There are several individuals who have made special contributions that need to have individual mention. Specifically, our thanks go to Larry Taylor, Lisa Dawes-Strachota, and Marc Diebold, who are responsible for many of the historical images; to Jane Bielawski, Jim Gilday, and Joan Lekens, who loaned us family albums; and Dr. Jerry Leer, who provided the cover picture and became a one-man cheering squad for our work.

Of course, without our late fathers, James Hillman and Jack Murphy, we would have never experienced any of the events that made the memories leading to this effort to preserve the history of these magical places of our youth. Finally, thanks to Kathy and Rita for their love and encouragement in this work and in life every day.

INTRODUCTION

While the social and recreational clubs of Indianapolis directly and indirectly affected the lives of every resident, the clubs also impacted national and international political agendas. For the most part, these clubs are gone. Some facilities still exist, but they operate in much different ways than the clubs of years past.

Arising from the "old money" social and political networks of the powerful elite and culturally relevant were the city clubs, organizations like the Columbia Club, the Indianapolis Athletic Club, and the Propyleaum, the oldest private club in the United States owned and operated by and for women. These organizations had exclusive membership limited by family name, political and legal clout, and economic supremacy. The city clubs were havens for the affluent, where members could relax, avoid the pressures of public scrutiny, and escape the opposite sex, or at least their spouses. At the male-dominated clubs, the men were free to socialize and network, eat, drink, maybe smoke a cigar, and play some billiards or gamble. Women's roles were passive in the male clubs but active in their own organizations, where they played cards, engaged in civic formalities, had tea, and, of course, influenced their husbands behind closed doors. But regardless of gender, all members were integral in dictating political platforms, influencing legal decisions, promoting cultural and social change, and literally ensuring the growth and development of Indiana's largest city.

By the close of the 1800s, traditional country clubs were taking root in Indianapolis; the first proper club was simply named the Country Club, originally located on the grounds of the current Woodstock Club. Established in 1891, the clubhouse burned to the ground in 1914. Some members saw that as an opportunity to move farther away from the expanding heart of Indianapolis and develop a world-class golfing facility by locating in a rural area on the outskirts of northwest Marion County, the present location of the Country Club of Indianapolis. Other members remained on the original club site and formed what is now the Woodstock Club.

Golf was the sport that defined the refined man of leisure. Other country clubs specializing in golf followed the origination of the Country Club, most notably Highland Golf and Country Club (1908), Broadmoor Country Club (1921), Meridian Hills Country Club (1923), Avalon Hills Country Club, renamed Hillcrest Country Club (1926), and Indian Lake Country Club (1928). While the majority of country clubs centered around their pristine golf courses (public golfing was simply not available, or the facilities were shabby or of poor design), clubs like Avalon Hills began as a swimming facility, later adding golf. Woodstock, while featuring golf, is better known for tennis and is known as well for introducing platform tennis to Indianapolis.

At the beginning of the 20th century, public swimming pools were emerging but were often lacking in proper sanitation. From donated land in the heart of downtown Indianapolis, the first public pool was located at Delaware and South Streets. On the outskirts of Indianapolis, the most significant public pool was built at White City Amusement Park in Broad Ripple Village, the location of the current city-owned Broad Ripple Park. The success of the northern Broad Ripple pool enticed future large semiprivate swimming developments, like Westlake Beach Club to the west and Longacre Park to the south.

With the calm between the strife of the two world wars, the Riviera Club entered the Indianapolis social club scene in 1933 and became a prototype for a new breed of socializing, the family recreational club. Originating as a world-class swimming facility, the club produced a number of swimming Olympians and regional, national, and international competitors. Supplementing aquatics, the club also offered a picnic area, basketball court, tennis courts, and formal dining facilities (no alcohol served) and later added an indoor pool, gymnasium, and health and exercise amenities.

After World War II, Americans experienced an increase in leisure time, but they did not necessarily have the stature to be invited to join the exclusive country clubs; there was also a renewed cultural emphasis on the importance of the family. Several family recreational clubs were built to meet a middle-class demand for club life, including Miramar (1955), Speedway Recreational Club, later renamed Westwood (1956), Devon Country Club (1956), Olympia (1958), Dolphin (1959), Westchester (1961), and a handful of other private and subdivision-neighborhood pools. While most of these facilities were focused on tennis, picnicking, swimming, and local social events, including dances, weddings, and class reunions, a handful of clubs, like the Heather Hills Country Club (now the semiprivate Maple Creek Country Club), also offered golf.

While family recreational clubs flourished into the 1970s, most were beginning to experience a fade of popularity, partially due to changing social protocol and varied competition for leisure time. Of the swim clubs, only a few have survived, including the Riviera, Devon, and Westchester. While the recreational clubs' viability was in decline, the city clubs and traditional country clubs also had to adapt to challenging times, including court mandates prohibiting segregation. Many built new clubhouse facilities, adjusted their membership criteria, and altered their social and recreational offerings, while a few, including the prestigious Indianapolis Athletic Club, were eventually forced to close.

And what does the future hold? With increasing property taxes, stagnation and decline of membership candidates, the costs associated with club maintenance and updating facilities, changing consumer expectations, competition from chain health clubs, and a multitude of other concerns, many of the remaining social clubs will continue to struggle in their present state. In our discussions with club members and managers we have heard talk of established clubs merging, private facilities becoming semiprivate, or retrenchment into the former truly exclusive nature of years past.

From the pomp and circumstance of Queen Marie of Romania visiting the Columbia Club, to Hoosier poet James Whitcomb Riley and Pres. Benjamin Harrison dining at the Country Club of Indianapolis, to Bob Hope golfing at Broadmoor and Olympian Becky Collins swimming at the Riviera, times have changed. Within the following pages, we will attempt to capture the social atmosphere and lifestyles of the social clubs of Indianapolis. In no way is this work to be considered as comprehensive. It is limited to private and semiprivate Marion County social and recreational clubs that were housed in brick and mortar facilities and by our ability to secure quality images. While many fondly remember the clubs of Indianapolis, most did not take their cameras to the club for a swim or round of golf. We found that family photographs were misplaced, lost, or destroyed, and newspaper and club archives are often nonexistent or severely incomplete. Because the clubs occupied a time in recent history, historical societies have not accumulated adequate Indianapolis social club holdings.

But the water still sparkles at the Devon Country Club pool. The well-manicured golf course at Meridian Hills is still a busy place, perfect pyramids of golf balls awaiting the members at the driving range. The Cascade Room at the Columbia Club continues to provide fine dining for the political and social movers and shakers of Indianapolis. And the rest of us, either inside or outside the exclusive gates of the social clubs of Indianapolis, cherish our memories of a different time.

One

THE CITY CLUBS

In the galaxy of cities, Indianapolis shares with only a few others the distinction of being designed from the outset as a capital city. The original plan for the mile-square downtown district centers around a circle that originally was planned to be the governor's residence. The quadrants of the center city are purpose driven; the west is reserved for the state capitol, to the east are the city and county government buildings and central market, the north houses the federal post office and courthouse, and the south is devoted to the main highway and railroad terminals.

Largely because of this plan, the center city immediately became a magnet for attorneys and politicians, who had court and government business, and the principal merchants, who needed the railroads and the central market. Where the government and the merchants are, the bankers are sure to follow, and where the railroads are, the industrialists will inevitably be drawn. So it was, that while still a young city, the downtown became the center of business and social activity.

The downtown population of the wealthy and powerful wanted and needed places to interact, to share common ideas, and to formulate business and political deals outside of public scrutiny. They also wanted places to gather for political, recreational, and social purposes, places that adequately demonstrated very clearly that they constituted the establishment class of the city.

Out of these desires and needs grew first the political clubs, soon followed by the ethnic and athletic clubs. In time, all these original clubs re-created themselves as private gathering places for the gentlemen to meet for drinks, a game of billiards, and some serious discussions of pending business, financial, and political plans. The women also formed a club of their own to promote literary, artistic, and social causes.

Each of the city clubs had its own distinctive flavor, but their common purpose was the provision of exclusive retreats in the heart of the city and places for the conduct of premier social events.

The Columbia Club, which was originally formed as a Republican marching society, is shown here at the 1892 Republican National Convention at Minneapolis, Minnesota. In an age before the availability of mass media advertising, the political marching societies were a vehicle to generate public attention for candidates and parties. Even at this early date, the Indianapolis political organizations were exerting influence on a national level. (The Columbia Club Foundation.)

As the city clubs matured, they began to establish permanent facilities in buildings constructed especially for their purposes. This view of the center circle shows the first clubhouse of the Columbia Club, located next to Christ Church Cathedral. The exquisite structure and its location at the very center of the city speak to the importance the city clubs were gaining in the society. (The Columbia Club Foundation.)

10

The Marion Club was an early example of the political clubs seen today. These postcard views from 1903 show the downtown clubhouse/headquarters it established to provide a place for meetings, a lounge and gathering place for members to meet and discuss local and national political affairs, and office space to operate such functions as the voter registration campaign illustrated below. Membership in a club such as this was a way to exert political influence and to be actively involved in election campaigns. Old political lore speaks of deals made in "smoke filled rooms"; these clubs were the buildings where those rooms were located. (Authors' collection.)

Marion Club, Indianapolis, Ind.

Your Last Opportunity to Register is on Monday, October 6th

You live in Ward _7_ Precinct _6_ and you register at

1835 N. New Jersey St.

between the hours of 6 a. m. and 9 p. m. on Monday, October 6th.

It is your duty as a member of the MARION CLUB to register and see that your Republican neighbors do the same.

MARION CLUB ELECTIONS COMMITTEE
SCHUYLER A. HAAS, Chairman

PUT THIS CARD IN YOUR POCKET AS A REMINDER

P. S.   Please notify Marion Club office of any change in your residence or business address within the last year.

A 1910 view from the steps of the monument, now located on the circle, shows the first clubhouse of the Columbia Club, located next to Christ Church Cathedral. The building shown here was home to a growing club that would soon find a need to expand. (The Columbia Club Foundation.)

When expanded facilities were required to accommodate the growing membership, the Columbia Club elected to retain its prominent Monument Circle location, demolishing the first clubhouse and constructing a fine new building on the lot. The new structure fairly exudes the image of establishment and prestige. In this 1917 postcard view, a group of liverymen pose at the entrance to the new clubhouse. (Authors' collection.)

The Columbia Club continued to grow and expand its role as a prominent meeting place for business and political interests as well as becoming one of the most prestigious locations for social events. The club wanted to add sleeping accommodations for prominent visitors, traveling members of similar clubs in other cities, and for the state legislators who were required to be in Indianapolis for meetings of the Indiana General Assembly. So the second clubhouse, like the first, was demolished and replaced by another new structure. Although a bit less ornate on the exterior, this new building boasted the finest appointments and greatly expanded the club's services to members and guests. Although a number of renovations over the years have modernized the hotel area and added services, care has been taken to preserve the atmosphere and appointments of establishment and exclusivity. (The Columbia Club Foundation.)

A few blocks north of the circle on Meridian Street, a group of prominent businessmen, with an interest in sports, formed the Indianapolis Athletic Club. While the club building did include a lounge and fine dining and banquet facilities, much of the building was devoted to an indoor swimming pool, a gymnasium, handball and squash courts, and exercise facilities. (Indianapolis Athletic Club.)

These seven men were employed in 1926 to promote the health of Indianapolis Athletic Club members and to improve their sporting abilities. They are, from left to right, Prof. Nestor LeMaire, fencing instructor; Claude Powers, head of the Turkish bath department; Howard Wiggam, boxing instructor; Pep Krantz, athletic director; William Bechstein, swimming instructor; Ray Falls, wrestling instructor; and Wally Nelson, golf professional. (Indianapolis Athletic Club.)

14

The year-round facility and excellent coaching staff at the Indianapolis Athletic Club produced a number of championship swimmers over the years. In this 1960 photograph, Mike Troy (left) celebrates with a teammate after breaking an Amateur Athletic Union record in national competition. (Indianapolis Athletic Club.)

The interest in sports and the excellent indoor pool facility made the athletic club a natural for the development of competitive swimming teams and training programs. For young swimmers, summers were spent at the outdoor pools of the many area clubs, with the prospect of "moving up" to the athletic club team for the winter season. This 1970 swim team includes numerous swimmers from other area clubs. (Marc Diebold.)

The championship swimmers were not just a function of the facility and coaching staff but also depended on the swimmers' own dedication to practice. In this 1982 photograph, a group of swimmers is seen at an early-morning practice session working on swimming skills before heading to school for the day. (Indianapolis Athletic Club.)

The civic activities of the Indianapolis Athletic Club included participation in the Buy-A-Plane bond sales effort during World War II. The club was so successful in this effort that two military aircraft were named for the club. Over the years, the members of the city clubs were consistently leaders in contributing to civic and social causes. (Indianapolis Athletic Club.)

As the Indianapolis Athletic Club celebrated 50 years, some of the members and guests arrived in a style reminiscent of the time when the city clubs were the principal locations for major social events. Chauffeured limousines were a common sight at these clubs in the 1920s and 1930s. (Indianapolis Athletic Club.)

While the gentlemen were enjoying the amenities of the Indianapolis Athletic Club, it was easy to forget that while the name might be *club*, these facilities were substantial business operations. There were dues to be collected, billing for member services, and general bills to be paid. Mary Rankin was a part of the business staff that managed the club operations in the 1950s. (Jim Gilday.)

While the front entrance was appointed with ornate fixtures and furnishings to properly accommodate the members, the office staff was generally found in a location seldom, if ever, seen by the members. Yet without the diligence of the many clerical workers, the services the members so treasured would not have been possible. (Meridian Hills Country Club.)

Although the city clubs developed primarily as men's organizations, a group of women saw a need for facilities to house a number of women's groups, including arts, music, and social benefit programs. The group organized the Propylaeum for this purpose and constructed a building on Vermont Street in 1891. Pictured here in 1921, the sculpted stone shows the soot from the downtown coal-fired power plant. (Indiana State Library.)

After World War I, the city decided to establish a central park area consisting of a number of war memorials and open space. The original Propylaeum building was acquired by the city and razed for the new park. The organization then purchased a large residential property, also dating from 1891, on North Delaware Street. The residence itself, seen above, provided space for all the club's functions and offered rooming facilities for single ladies for several years. Also on the property is a large carriage house structure that provided the first home for the Indianapolis Children's Museum. The Propylaeum remains a vital and active participant in the social life of Indianapolis. The facility hosts a number of community events and is one of the premier locations in the city for formal social gatherings. (Authors' collection.)

"DAS DEUTSCHE HAUS." INDIANAPOLIS, IND.

Just as the political, business, and sports interests had brought together the founders of the Columbia and Indianapolis Athletic Clubs, the cultural affinity of the large population of German descent resulted in the establishment of organizations that catered to the dining, social, and sports interests of this group. The postcard above pictures "Das Deutsche Haus," later named the Athenaeum, located on the eastern edge of the downtown area. The building was constructed in stages from 1893 through 1898 in a German Renaissance style. The exterior features sculpted terra-cotta and limestone by local artist Alexander Sangernebo. The building included a gymnasium, athletic facilities, and dining and banquet rooms. Among the activities of the organization was the preservation of traditional music through various performing groups such as the Athenian Minstrels, shown below in a 1912 group photograph. (Above, authors' collection; below, Mike Somsel.)

Maennerchor Club, Indianapolis, Ind.

Similar to the Athenaeum, other clubs were created to provide community meeting and activity places for the increasingly prosperous immigrant communities. The Mannerchor Club (above) and the Southside Turners Hall (below) were examples of facilities that provided dining, meeting, and sports in the neighborhoods surrounding the downtown area. The typical construction of these buildings featured the European brick and sculptured-stone style. The buildings were large enough to house a gymnasium, other sports facilities, and large gathering spaces. They became a hub of neighborhood activity, assembling sports teams to compete against the other clubs and hosting neighborhood festivals and weddings. They served not only as neighborhood centers but also helped to preserve much of the cultural heritage the immigrant families had brought to Indianapolis. (Authors' collection.)

One group of sports enthusiasts decided to take advantage of the city's location on the White River and established the Canoe Club on the near northwest side of the downtown area. The club constructed a large clubhouse that provided dining and meeting space and built dock and canoe storage facilities at the waterfront, as seen in this 1908 postcard view. (Authors' collection.)

The first building constructed by the Canoe Club is seen here from the White River Parkway side. As with most waterfront structures, the street side is far less impressive than the waterfront side. Seen from the street, the structure appears much as a typical large home of the time. The docks and boating area are hidden from public view by the clubhouse itself. (Indiana State Library.)

Canoe Club, Indianapolis, Ind.

The Canoe Club's new clubhouse building is seen in this 1910 postcard (above) from the entrance along the White River Parkway. The building is seen below under construction in the winter months. The city eventually acquired the property, and the 1910 building now serves as the home of the Indianapolis Municipal Gardens. While catering to the same clientele as the downtown city clubs, the Canoe Club facilities were less formal in nature and centered on leisurely time spent on the water. While being considered a city club by the members, this club was an indicator of the growing movement to establish the country clubs with their focus on outdoor activities away from the commercial center of the city. (Above, authors' collection; below, Indiana State Library.)

As the city clubs flourished, so did the commercial aspects of the city itself. By the early part of the 20th century, Indianapolis was not only the state capital but was also the center of the American automobile industry and the associated manufacturing plants. Power was provided by steam, gas, and electricity that were generated in large coal-fired power plants located along the near downtown riverfront. As seen in this photograph of the state capitol, downtown Indianapolis, like other large cities, was not a picturesque place. The downtown locations of the city clubs still spoke to their station in society, and they were still prime locations for social and political events, but downtown Indianapolis was no longer the place for recreation. The winds of change blew away from the center of the city and became gentle breezes in the trees of the country clubs. Soon the gentlemen's afternoon drink and cigar would be in a lounge overlooking a golf course, and "going to the club" would have a new meaning. (Authors' collection.)

Two

WHERE HISTORY AND TRADITION MEET

The Columbia Club (1889) is one of the most photographed facilities in Indianapolis. Aside from the prime Monument Circle location and magnificent architecture, the Columbia Club's membership has included many of Indianapolis's most wealthy and powerful visionaries. The Columbia Club has hosted many prestigious events and guests, including every Republican president since Pres. Benjamin Harrison.

The Columbia Club began from a contingent of distinguished citizens who dawned robes and marched in effort to elect Benjamin Harrison to office. The Harrison Marching Society was prominent, welcoming all national Republican dignitaries to Indianapolis. It was the society's political notoriety that prompted ambition to secure a permanent clubhouse. Patiently pursuing prime real estate, the society secured its first of three facilities with frontage on what was to become Monument Circle. In 1889, at the former residence of William H. Morrison, the Columbia Club had a home.

The need for facility expansion and enhancements soon emerged. The Columbia Club would eventually raze the Morrison House and construct a new clubhouse, dedicated on New Year's Eve 1890, followed by construction of an even more spectacular facility in 1925.

Club treasures include numerous pieces of art and artifacts. There is a vast collection of paintings, including impressive T. C. Steele works. The Marott Trophy, one of the world's most expensive, is encased in the main lobby, the result of years of sports rivalry with the primarily Democratic Indianapolis Athletic Club. On display is the Lincoln Eagle that traveled in Pres. Abraham Lincoln's funeral procession. There is a marble-top table presented by President Harrison to the club in 1893.

With firm Republican roots, the Columbia Club of today is diverse, encompassing the spectrum of political ideologies, with their legacy poised to support future generations of leaders in relevance and style. Nearly 2,000 current members enjoy the private and personable ambiance of the club, and with 97 overnight rooms, a state-of-the-art fitness center, conference rooms, dining, lounge facilities, and other amenities, the Columbia Club remains the social centerpiece of Indianapolis. The club was placed on the National Register of Historic Places in 1983.

The initial meeting of the primary stockholders of the Columbia Club occurred on February 6, 1889. From the second-floor meeting area of the When Building on North Pennsylvania Street, plans were solidified, and papers of incorporation were filed, just a week later, with the recorder's office in Indianapolis. (The Columbia Club Foundation.)

With firm cornerstones of conservatism, prestige, and privacy, the Columbia Club has hosted every Republican president, either as a president or candidate, since the term of Pres. Benjamin Harrison (1889–1893), and, as of this publication, continuing through Pres. George W. Bush (2001–2009). Pres. Theodore Roosevelt accepted honorary membership in the club on November 1, 1901. (The Columbia Club Foundation.)

Pres. William Howard Taft visited the Columbia Club on July 4, 1911, as the guest of former vice president Charles and Cornelia Fairbanks. He received a supportive welcome by a crowd surrounding Monument Circle. Once inside the clubhouse, President Taft enjoyed a patriotic luncheon hosted by club president Louis F. Smith. Later that day, visits to celebrations at Washington Park and the Indiana State Fairgrounds were scheduled, the latter being sponsored by Indianapolis railroad workers. That evening President Taft was the keynote speaker at a dinner at the Marion Club, which was his primary purpose in visiting Indianapolis. (The Columbia Club Foundation.)

Charles Evans Hughes and Charles Fairbanks, the 1916 Republican presidential ticket, enjoy the privacy of a chat on the Fairbanks veranda. The race motivated many Columbians to take a specially commissioned Fairbanks booster train to Chicago, once again demonstrating the Columbia Club's political activism, even if the eventual outcome was not the desired result. (The Columbia Club Foundation.)

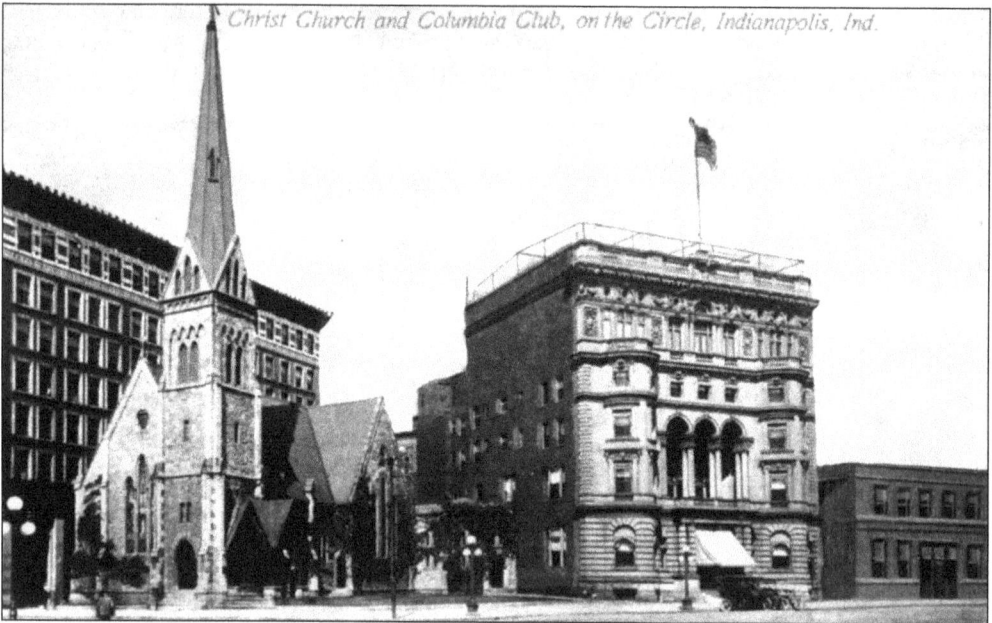

This 1920 postcard view shows the Columbia Club's second clubhouse next to Christ Church Cathedral. The club became the largest Republican club in the Midwest. This increase in membership was attributed to creative canvassing and recruitment of Indiana's prominent Republicans. The campaign included lowering nonresident fees, including initiation costs, waiving the required stock purchase, and freezing annual dues. The club's membership increased 60 percent, causing the current facilities to become inadequate. (Authors' collection.)

With the William H. Morrison residence, the first home of the Columbia Club, long gone, the nearly quarter-century-old second clubhouse was razed in 1924; the interim facilities were relocated to the Marion Club on North Meridian Street. During early summer, the historic cornerstone was opened and the contents examined by (left to right) an unknown participant, directors Fred C. Gardner and Frank Butler, and club president Arthur E. Bradshaw. Construction began on the third clubhouse and is pictured in a construction photograph dated September 15, 1924. The original 1899 cornerstone artifacts joined newly added 1924 items, such as a current club history and newspapers, and all were encased into the new construction on October 14, 1924. (The Columbia Club Foundation.)

COLUMBIA CLUB
WM. P. JUNGCLAUS CO.
Contractors
Indianapolis, Indiana

Col. Charles A. Lindbergh visited the Columbia Club on August 9, 1927, to promote the wonders and realities of aviation. Lindbergh, noted for his solo airplane flight over the Atlantic, was considered a true American hero. During his visit, a parade around Monument Circle was conducted, as well as a formal dinner where he was presented with an honorary club membership. During this event, attended by nearly 600 Columbians, Lindbergh received three standing ovations by an audience not easily awestruck. Amelia Earhart, another hero of aviation, also visited the club, receiving honor and respect from the Columbians, regardless of her gender. Known as the place to be seen, the Columbia Club hosted several celebrities in 1927, including Gen. John J. Pershing, Columbia University president Dr. Nicholas Murray, and Her Majesty Queen Marie of Romania, who arrived with her entourage aboard 12 railroad cars and filled the entire fifth floor of the club. (The Columbia Club Foundation.)

Having just hosted an extensive welcome for Her Majesty Queen Marie of Romania, a visit by His Majesty Crown Prince William of Sweden prompted yet another elaborate banquet and festivities. On October 12, 1927, the event, chaired by Columbian Wallace O. Lee, captivated the attention of Indiana, national, and international media. (The Columbia Club Foundation.)

During the winter of 1928–1929, jazz music flourished at the Columbia Club with the tunes of Bloomington's Hoagy Carmichael, composer of "Stardust" and "Georgia on My Mind." Joined by another icon, Nipper, the RCA Victor mascot, along with his orchestra, Carmichael was a mainstay at the club as the 1920s gave way to the approaching hardships of the next two decades. (The Columbia Club Foundation.)

In 1935, the six-foot-tall Marott Trophy found a permanent home at the Columbia Club. Developer George J. Marott was approached about donating a special prize for a best-out-of-10 interclub competition between the primarily Republican Columbia Club and the Democratic Indianapolis Athletic Club. Jeweler C. B. Dyer, under the guidance of Marott, designed a magnificent bounty of 60 ounces of gold, 600 ounces of solid sterling silver, 200 full-cut diamonds, and to solidify its value, Marott added some of his wife's own jewelry. The Indianapolis Athletic Club would default on the tournament after only two wins to the Columbia Club's five wins. In 1940, the Columbia Club was presented with a Lincoln Eagle, a wood-carved treasure that traveled with Abraham Lincoln's funeral procession. The Columbia Club displays many priceless artifacts, including many original T. C. Steele artworks. (The Columbia Club Foundation.)

The April 15, 1940, festivities at the Columbia Club were known as Dewey Day. Nearly 700 Columbian ladies and their guests gathered to honor Thomas E. Dewey's wife at a stately luncheon. Thomas E. Dewey would become the Republican presidential nominee in both 1944 and 1948. This gathering of women remains the largest in the history of the club. (The Columbia Club Foundation.)

Our Anniversary Party

THE ANNUAL
BEEFSTEAK DINNER

Friday, March 7th
6:30 P. M.

Governor Dwight H. Green, of Illinois,
as Guest Speaker

Gala Imported

All-Girl Show

★

With The Beefsteaks
and Frog Legs

★

The Club's 25-Year
"Veterans" will be Honor-
Guests at Reserved Tables

The Columbians liked to have fun. The Beefsteak Dinner on March 7, 1941, featured speaker Illinois governor Dwight H. Green, a transplanted Hoosier. As U.S. district attorney, Governor Green presented the government's evidence against "Scarface," landing Al Capone in the big house of Alcatraz. As if that was not enough excitement for the evening, an expensive, imported all-girl show was presented to the club's discriminating gentlemen. (The Columbia Club Foundation.)

Through the years, the Columbia Club would often decorate the outside of the clubhouse with welcoming banners for political candidates. Columbian Wendell Willkie, Republican presidential nominee, visited the club for a campaign conference on September 12, 1940. Whenever Willkie came to Indiana, he drew large crowds, especially when he visited his birthplace, Elwood, to receive presidential nomination notification on August 17, 1940; over 1,000 Columbians witnessed the historic August ceremony. The club benefited from the Willkie campaign, not just from media exposure but from the dollars spent by the campaign and nomination committee staying at the Columbia Club. While Willkie eventually lost to Pres. Franklin D. Roosevelt, he became a special envoy for the president, traveling around the world to visit U.S. allies and writing about his experiences in the book *One World*, published in 1943. (The Columbia Club Foundation.)

Day clerk Paul Kane saw many famous faces arrive as guests of the club in the 1950s. While Kane no longer works the front desk, this area of the club otherwise looks much as it did in the early years. Rich and famous guests were numerous, including the talented Clark Gable, depicted as he enters the club for the Borg-Warner prerace party in 1950. Other early-1950s visitors included businessman J. C. Penny, actress Loretta Young, Sen. Robert A. Taft (1951), Sen. Everett Dickson (1951 and 1952), United States treasurer Ivy Baker Priest, entertainers Rudy Vallee and Mel Torme (1953), Pres. Dwight D. Eisenhower (1954), and a handful of others. (The Columbia Club Foundation.)

As far as most Columbians were concerned, Dwight D. Eisenhower was to be the underdog to William Howard Taft at the 1952 Republican Convention. Regardless, when Eisenhower came to Indianapolis in September 1952, he was warmly greeted with banners and the subtlety of a blimp. Soon-to-be-president Eisenhower conducted a major campaign speech during this trip. Returning to the club a few years later as President Eisenhower, he met with Congressman Charles Halleck and conferred during festivities to honor Indiana's 1954 congressional delegation. (The Columbia Club Foundation.)

Revisiting the club's roots as the Harrison Marching Society, the marching Columbians paraded from the union station to the club on October 20, 1964. This torchlight occasion, led by former governor Harold Handley (right) and Dr. Max S. Norris, occurred prior to their annual Beefsteak Dinner and was in celebration of the club's 75th anniversary. (The Columbia Club Foundation.)

Indianapolis mayor and future U.S. senator, Columbian Richard G. Lugar was a prolific speaker around the club. As a result of his groundbreaking leadership, including UniGov, which rolled most of Marion County into Indianapolis, his urban renewal projects, and his close relationships with national leadership, the club once again became an important sounding board on national political issues. (Columbia Club Foundation.)

A welcoming banner was stretched across the front windows of the Columbia Club to acknowledge Pres. Richard Nixon and wife Pat campaigning in Indianapolis on September 12, 1968. Along with the majority of club members, nearly 25,000 general supporters gathered at Monument Circle. Mayor Richard G. Lugar was often referred to as President Nixon's favorite mayor. Lugar was young, full of energy and ambition, and embodied all that was progressive in the Republican Party. The Columbia Club was supportive in Lugar's near cometlike political assent. Mayor Lugar is photographed at the club with President Nixon in 1970, when Nixon's urban affairs committee held its first meeting outside Washington. (The Columbia Club Foundation.)

Keeping with tradition in the 1970s, Pres. Gerald Ford visited and spoke at the club. Another political power broker, Sen. Barry Goldwater is pictured with, from left to right, Columbian Bar Bumpers Bill Chambers and Ron Gaston and Columbian Ron Corn. During the early part of this decade, the club hosted a variety of notables, including *Apollo 12* astronauts Pete Conrad and Dick Gordon (1970), actress Joan Crawford (1970), broadcasting executive Robert B. McConnell (1971), Lord and Lady Polwarth of Scotland (1971), jazz entertainer Pete Fountain (1973), Republican national chairman George H. W. Bush (1973), Texan John B. Connally (1974), and several other celebrities. (The Columbia Club Foundation.)

Continuing as Indianapolis's grand host, famous individuals flocked to enjoy the privacy and prestige of the rapidly diversifying Columbia Club well into the 1970s and 1980s. Comedienne Phyllis Diller enjoyed a drink at the club in 1976. Other celebrities sighted in 1976 included sports artist LeRoy Neiman, and, in town for the Bob Hope Birthday Party to benefit the United Services Organizations, Gen. James Doolittle, Charlie Pride, Don Knotts, Shirley Jones, and of course Bob Hope. Mike Schaefer, Ruth Musgrave, and David Rickey stand watch over weatherman Willard Scott and Hoosier actress Joyce DeWitt. The variety of national personalities that have enjoyed the club is ongoing. (The Columbia Club Foundation.)

It was a grand and glorious night filling two complete floors of the Columbia Club. Distinguished actor and California governor Ronald Reagan was the 1979 Beefsteak Dinner speaker. Reagan is seen informally greeting fellow Columbians prior to receiving a gold Columbia Club membership card later that evening. The honorary membership was a nice complement to his additional gifts, jellybeans and a weed whacker device to use at his California ranch. Being the center of attention, Reagan appeared in high spirits. Several Columbians could be heard discussing Reagan's political future. The soon-to-be president is also pictured with Keith Bullen. (The Columbia Club Foundation.)

In the late 1970s, native Hoosier and cohost of NBC's *Today Show,* Jane Pauley spoke at the Columbia Club's Advertisement Club luncheon. Pauley discussed her career and life after Indiana. Relevant entertainment speakers were becoming popular with Columbians. Toward the conclusion of the 1970s, Indiana University's Lee Corso, Jeane Dixon, and Norman Vincent Peale were just a few professionals offering their motivational wisdom to members. (The Columbia Club Foundation.)

Pres. Benjamin Harrison's grandson William Henry Harrison accepted an invitation to the President's Ball of 1981. Harrison traveled from Wyoming to speak, telling lively stories about the Harrison family. The club's historical roots were on the minds of the Columbia Club's leaders as they proceeded to gain listing on the National Register of Historic Places, and designation was bestowed upon the club on February 12, 1983. (The Columbia Club Foundation.)

Holidays meant special family times at the club. Aside from the political overtones surrounding Fourth of July celebrations, the club provided members opportunities to relax and celebrate New Year's, Easter, Halloween, Christmas, and other holidays. Special parties and events, often themed, helped to reduce the stress associated with politics, government, and business. Pictured is a special visit by the Easter Bunny to the eager children of Columbians, as well as former Indianapolis mayor William Hudnut, standing in front of the club, sporting green tights in 1987. Columbian leprechaun Hudnut is probably searching for a pot of gold for the City of Indianapolis after participating in the annual St. Patrick's Day parade, sponsored by the rival Indianapolis Athletic Club. (The Columbia Club Foundation.)

Competitions have always been a source of Columbia Club pride. The club sponsored the United States Rowing Association 1987 National Regatta Championships on the reservoir at Eagle Creek. In full club insignia uniforms, the rowing members of the club pose for a 1988 photograph. It does not seem to bother Columbians that they are living in the largest American city with the smallest bodies of water. (The Columbia Club Foundation.)

The Columbia Club
A Distinguished Tradition Since 1889

The Columbia Club continues to serve not only Republicans, membership is diverse, and varied political affiliations are represented. Harry S. New is credited with naming the club. *Columbia* refers to the "Gem of the Ocean" or Uncle Sam's handmaiden, and a handmaiden's cap is still a part of the corporate logo of the Columbia Club, "a distinguished tradition since 1889." (The Columbia Club Foundation.)

Three

THE COUNTRY CLUBS

By the end of the 19th century, Indianapolis was developing not only as an industrial, commercial, and political city, but there was a growing cosmopolitan trend. The same group that constituted the membership of the city clubs was now looking to enjoy such outdoor activities as riding and polo, golf, tennis, and swimming. Obviously, these activities required considerable space that was only available on the outskirts of the city.

The first country club was established on farmland that was a then far distant three miles from the city center. Although the location was along a canal and could be accessed by walking or bicycling along the towpath, a proper arrival at the club required sufficient means to either own or hire a carriage. The location provided not only the space for outdoor activities but also a measure of privacy and exclusivity.

The early country clubs were all formed by small numbers of individuals wealthy enough to purchase the capital stock in the form of memberships to fund the purchase of the land and construction of the clubhouse and a golf course. Given that many began with less than 100 members, clearly these were the private playgrounds of the wealthy.

By the beginning of the 20th century, the country clubs were expanding in number and facilities. The country clubs were the place to enjoy fine dining on a daily basis, the place to entertain important clients, and the place to meet one's peers in an exclusive environment. Membership in a club was a symbol of acceptance in the upper class, and the clubs became the place to be and be seen.

Some years after the original clubs, a new trend developed to incorporate a country club facility into the development of new housing additions. Membership in these clubs was restricted to those who purchased property and built homes in the development. In fact, a membership in the club often was a part of the purchase of the land itself, as was the requirement to pay ongoing dues to support the club operations.

Country Club,
Indanapolis, Ind.

In 1891, a group of businessmen gathered and formed the first country club in the Indianapolis area. Located along the Central Canal at Thirty-eighth Street, it was first known as simply the Country Club. This 1909 postcard shows the fine clubhouse that was constructed in 1905. The club offered nine holes of golf, tennis, and even had a swimming pool for the members to enjoy. The location was near the city for the convenience of the members but distant enough that a substantial level of privacy was assured. The club's amenities provided fine dining, social events, and comfortable lounges and card rooms, in addition to the outdoor sports facilities. The club flourished in this location until a devastating fire in 1914 hastened an already planned move to a larger space west of the city. (Above, authors' collection; below, Country Club of Indianapolis.)

Prior to the 1914 fire, a large parcel had been purchased west of the city to construct a new and larger golf course and club facility. The new location, opened in October 1914, was renamed the Country Club of Indianapolis and included a large clubhouse, tennis and swimming facilities, and an 18-hole golf course designed by William Diddel. (Country Club of Indianapolis.)

The golf course at the Country Club of Indianapolis has hosted a number of amateur and professional championship events, including the 26th United States Women's Open Championship in 1978. Years of subtle changes and improvements, along with the maturing of the trees, have made this course an outstanding example of country club golfing at its best. (Country Club of Indianapolis.)

After the Country Club of Indianapolis completed the relocation from the original property, an interest grew in creating a new club on the existing property. Some stories claim that some members were offended by the idea of a bar at the new club, or worried about their children traveling so far out in the country on poor roads to get to the new club location. With a focus on more family-oriented activities, the Woodstock Club was formed. A new clubhouse, now the third on the property, was completed for the opening of the Woodstock Club in March 1916. In 1922, fire again struck the club, destroying much of the 1916 clubhouse, and again the building process was undertaken. The remains of the clubhouse were renovated and expanded, creating the clubhouse that serves the club today. (The Woodstock Club.)

In 1969, the United States Tennis Association moved the U.S. Clay Court Championships from Milwaukee to Indianapolis, and Woodstock was chosen to host this event. The Western Open tournament relocated to Cincinnati, and the Clay Court Championships replaced it on the summer social calendar every year from 1969 until 1974, when a lack of seating capacity forced the tournament to relocate to a larger venue. (The Woodstock Club.)

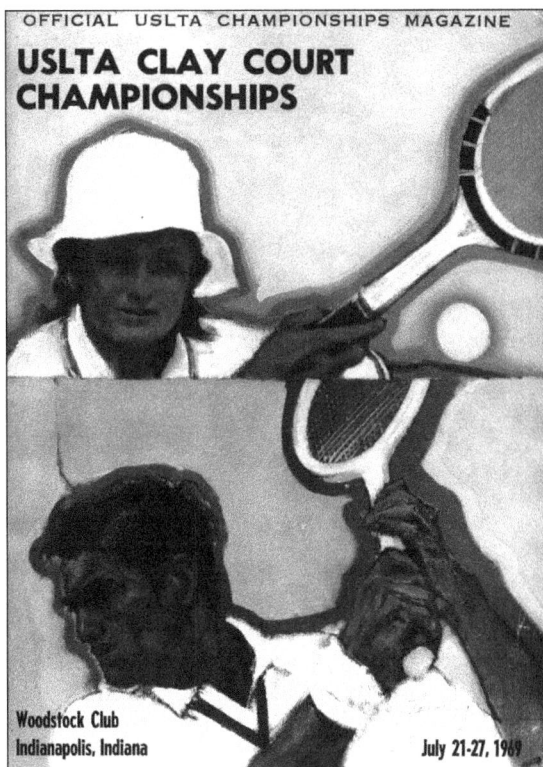

OFFICIAL USLTA CHAMPIONSHIPS MAGAZINE

USLTA CLAY COURT CHAMPIONSHIPS

Woodstock Club
Indianapolis, Indiana   July 21-27, 1969

In 1962, Woodstock introduced Indianapolis to a new form of tennis, paddle tennis. The game is played in a fenced enclosure on a wood or aluminum deck surface and can be played in all but the most inclement weather. The original courts have been upgraded, and a warming hut was added to provide for the players who favor the game in the fall and early spring. (The Woodstock Club.)

The Woodstock Club has long been known nationally as a premier tennis club. By the 1920s, Indianapolis was recognized as a tennis center and Woodstock was the top tennis venue in the city. The club featured seven clay courts, with two being designed especially for championship play. The club hosted the Western Open, the oldest amateur tennis tournament in the United

TERN TENNIS CHAMPIONSHIP
OCK CLUB ─── INDIANAPOLIS
JUNE - 21 - 28 - 1925

States, every other year from 1922 to 1965 and every year from 1966 to 1968. The Western Open was the social event of the summer. Woodstock has been selected by *Tennis* magazine as one of the top 50 outdoor tennis clubs in the United States. (The Woodstock Club.)

Befitting the major social event of the summer season, the Woodstock grounds were immaculately groomed, and the pool was decorated to become a virtual seaside resort. The poolside deck was the setting for luncheon with the players, officials, and guests from around the nation. The young ladies of the club were formed into a motor pool service to provide transportation to and from the local hotels, and teens would serve as ushers and usherettes. No effort was spared to not only make the visiting celebrities and players welcome but also to showcase the club and promote Indianapolis as a national tennis center. (The Woodstock Club.)

In 1903, a group of men formed the Highland Golf Club and entered into an arrangement with the City of Indianapolis to use "a portion of Riverside Park for golf purposes." The club members proceeded to construct a nine-hole course on the upland of what is today known as Coffin Golf Course. A shed on a nearby farm served as the clubhouse, and area farmers were commissioned to keep the land manicured when they were not busy with farmwork. In 1908, they were granted additional land and expanded the course to 18 holes. In 1919, the land was needed for a city park expansion, so the members formed the present Highland Golf and Country Club and acquired 144 acres from the Eastman estate. The club constructed a clubhouse, tennis and swimming facilities, and an 18-hole golf course designed by Willie Park Jr. The comfortable but elegant clubhouse has seen minor renovations, but it stands today as the sole example of the early country club style. (Highland Golf and Country Club.)

The Highland clubhouse pictured in 1929 sets a formal theme with its columns and arched windows. The clubhouse provides locker rooms, card and meeting rooms, a lounge, the men's grill, and formal dining and banquet facilities. The formal dining room on the second floor of the clubhouse overlooks the golf course, and there is a deck area on the roof for more outdoor dining and lounging. (Highland Golf and Country Club.)

In the 1920s, every activity at the club was a "dress up" event, even an outdoor dance over the July 4 holiday weekend. Although the venue was a canvas tent structure to provide shade from the afternoon sun, the ladies and gentlemen were all in proper attire to enjoy the holiday party. (Highland Golf and Country Club.)

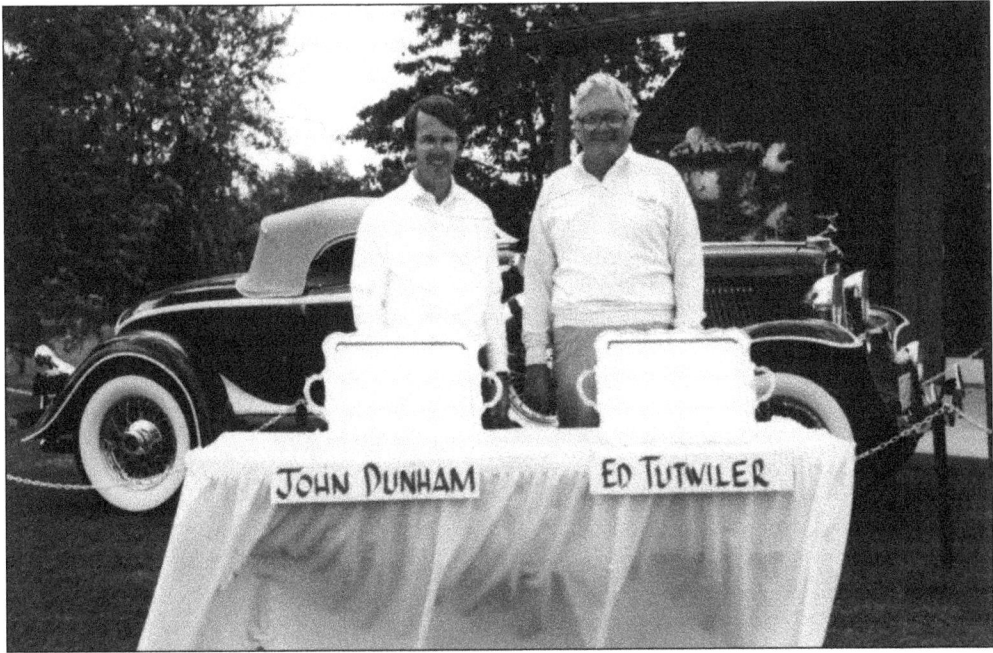

The Highland course has hosted a number of major tournaments, including the 1926 Western Open, the 1950 Indiana Amateur Championship, the 1955 Indiana Amateur Championship, and several Indiana Pro-Am Championships. Club professional John Dunham and local businessman Ed Tutwiler were regular winners of the pro-am events throughout the 1970s. (Dr. Jerry Leer.)

While having a drink at the club is a long-honored pastime, for many years each member purchased a bottle of his preferred liquor and had it kept at the bar for his use. To facilitate this, the club arranged to have liquors produced with their own label, only available to members at the club, as shown here by Dr. Jerry Leer, club historian. (Authors' collection.)

The very name *country club* evokes first and foremost the image of a golf course. Above is a view of the 18th hole at the Highland Golf and Country Club course designed by Willie Parks Jr. This exquisite 18-hole course was constructed after the club moved to its present location in 1919. Below is a view of a fairway at the Broadmoor Country Club, located a short distance west of Highland. This course was designed by Donald Ross and was constructed in 1923. Both courses have hosted numerous celebrity and championship events over the years and are recognized as among the best courses in the area. (Above, Highland Golf and Country Club; below, Broadmoor Country Club.)

In 1922, a group of businessmen from the Jewish community desired to have a country club that better suited their cultural customs, so they formed the Broadmoor Country Club on Kessler Boulevard, not far from the largest area synagogue. The club featured all the same amenities that the other clubs offered but tailored its event schedules, menus, and holiday celebrations to the Jewish membership. (Authors' collection.)

Broadmoor's outstanding golf course has hosted a number of tournaments and a variety of celebrity and charity events, which drew national attention. Such celebrities as comedian Bob Hope, shown here at a charity exhibition raising funds for the USO, have frequently played the course. (Helaine Simon.)

Arnold Palmer and Lee Trevino played at Broadmoor in one of the national professional tournaments the club hosted over the years. The club has not only hosted national events but is also a regular site for area amateur and charity tournaments and local fund-raising gatherings. (Broadmoor Country Club.)

The Broadmoor course hosted the men's Senior PGA Classic Tour each year from 1988 through 1993 and was also the site for the 2004 and 2005 men's and women's U.S. Open qualifiers and the 2006 Indiana State Amateur Championship. The course has been rated by *Golf Digest* as a top 100 classic course for many years. (Broadmoor Country Club.)

In July 1943, Broadmoor hosted an open house reception for approximately 500 servicemen. The event was held in memory of the late Fannie Lurvey (wife of David Lurvey), who helped to establish the USO center at the Kirshbaum Community Center. The soldiers and sailors took part in various sports for which members of the club supplied the equipment. One hundred cadets from Kirshbaum took part in the entertainment program. A chicken supper was served; there was swimming in the pool and dancing to the Variety Serenaders. The servicemen were brought to the club and returned to their station by a volunteer motor corps. (David Lurvey.)

In 1927, a group of investors planned an upscale residential development on the northeast side of the city named Avalon Hills. Included in the plan was a club facility for the buyers of the new homes. Originally opened in the spring of 1928, the club later opened its membership to persons who did not live in the Avalon Hills development, and it was renamed Hillcrest Country Club. (Authors' collection.)

In 1930, the club suffered a major fire that heavily damaged the original clubhouse building. However, the masonry construction was such that enough remained of the structure to allow it to be rebuilt, and some renovations were included in the rebuilding process. The reconstruction maintained the original structure well enough that the clubhouse was listed on the National Register of Historic Places in 2004. (Hillcrest Country Club.)

Another of the clubs to be established as a part of a housing development, the nine-hole course at Indian Lake Country Club was begun in 1928 as an amenity to a proposed residential development that also included a lake and riding stables. Unfortunately, the project had hardly reached an operational state when the Great Depression struck, and the club went into receivership. Two enterprising young golfers, Fred Kiesling and Hap Alyea, bought the property and brought it back to life first as a paid admission course and then restored it as a membership club operation in 1936. Once again, world events intervened. The economic struggles of World War II led to the property being sold for use as an Elks lodge. Following the war, a group of former members were able to acquire the property once again, and the present Indian Lake Country Club was incorporated in 1948. The golf course as it is pictured above has remained largely unchanged over the years. (Indian Lake Country Club.)

In front of the Indian Lake clubhouse in 1939, Nina Kiesling practices a putt under the watchful eyes of Milt Boatman, club manager; Marcus List, course superintendent; and Fred Kiesling, professional; while Jack Kiesling holds the flag. Fred was one of the men responsible for saving the property from receivership a few years earlier, and the family was a pillar of the club for many years. (Indian Lake Country Club.)

By 1949, Indian Lake had a women's golf team competing with other area country clubs on a regular basis. The area clubs all hosted luncheon golf outings on a regular basis, inviting the members of the other clubs to come for an afternoon of socializing and golf. The competition was friendly and rather informal, serving primarily as a way for each club to showcase their facilities. (Indian Lake Country Club.)

All the activities at the clubs were not golf related. In the 1970s, a particularly popular event was a luau-themed party around the club pool. Here the Indian Lake members are attired in their best Hawaiian costumes for an evening of food and fun at poolside. (Indian Lake Country Club.)

Begun in the 1960s, the Heather Hills residential development included a country club. The Heather Hills golf course was the first 18-hole golf course designed by Pete Dye, who went on to become a nationally recognized designer. The club also featured tennis and a pool and, like Avalon Hills and Indian Lake, was conceived as an amenity for the homeowners in the development. (Maple Creek Golf and Country Club.)

The Pete Dye–designed course soon became a popular location for numerous area charity and fund-raising events. These events, such as a fund-raiser for the Leukemia Foundation shown here, drew large numbers of local golfers and area celebrities to the club each summer and served as major social events for the club members and guests. (Maple Creek Golf and Country Club.)

Indiana University basketball coach Bobby Knight was a frequent celebrity guest golfer at the club. Knight was well known, not only for his basketball teams and high-profile public persona but also for his frequent appearances at area charity events. Playing a round of golf and getting one's picture taken with the popular coach was a benefit of club membership. (Maple Creek Golf and Country Club.)

As at other clubs in the 1970s, the luau party by the pool was a major summer attraction. At Heather Hills, the pool decorations and costumes were elaborate; a hog roast and buffet of tropical foods and, of course, a best-dressed contest were all part of the fun. At the 1973 luau party, the best-dressed award went to Chuck Preston and Mrs. Paul Stubbs, shown below with their prizes. The 1970s, and parties such as these, would prove to be a high point of club membership and popularity, not only at Heather Hills but at all the country clubs in the area. (Maple Creek Golf and Country Club.)

The country club was a popular destination for an evening of dining with friends and a place to hold such social events as wedding receptions in the formal rooms. In the club dining room, men were expected to be in a coat and tie, ladies wore dresses, the staff knew each member by name, and attentive service was expected. (Maple Creek Golf and Country Club.)

Heather Hills experienced a decline in membership, and the rising costs and competition from improved public golf courses led to the closure of the club in 2005. The property was acquired by investors who made some improvements and reopened the facilities as Maple Creek Golf and Country Club. The club today operates as a semiprivate facility, offering both membership and daily admission options. (Maple Creek Golf and Country Club.)

Four

FROM HUMBLE
BEGINNINGS

On the cornfields of the Spring Mill Road property known as the J. E. Morris farm, Meridian Hills Country Club was built on the strength of the Roaring Twenties economy. Because the location of the new Country Club of Indianapolis was located far west and the recently relocated Highland Country Club was reestablishing itself, the Meridian Hills Country Club germinated from a perceived geographical need; the nearest established competitor, the Woodstock Club, only offered golfers nine holes of play. In the spring of 1923, the club held its first organizational meeting at the Columbia Club.

The clubhouse, a remodeled quaint farmhouse, and a new William Diddel–designed 18-hole golf course, complete with donated periphery shrubs, became the original amenities provided to early members. Dining was promoted, but no alcohol was served, severely limiting popularity. Unique to Indianapolis country clubs, horse riding stables were added, eventually contracted to private enterprise, and then abandoned entirely in 1941. A small swimming pool was added in 1928 (replaced by an Olympic-size pool in 1964), and tennis courts were added in 1933 (updated and expanded in 1976). Ice-skating was initially allowed on the golf course ponds.

Meridian Hills Country Club faced a multitude of membership and financial struggles but ultimately prevailed. The club finally acquired property ownership in 1945. Although facility upgrades were sparse, the ultraconservative club finally opened a new, family-friendly clubhouse in 1950, adding revenue-generating alcohol to the menu. A new pro shop was built in 1953, and a new bathhouse was added. The golf course, modified by George Fazio, Peter Dye, and other member designers, gained recognition as one of the Midwest's finest.

Through the years, Meridian Hills Country Club has hosted many prestigious tournaments, including the U.S. Women's Amateur Championship. Several Meridian Hills lady golfers hold state golfing titles, while several male members have won Indiana state amateur titles, including Dale Morey, John David, and Ed Tutwiler. Meridian Hills' membership has included several golfers who have been elected to the Indiana Golf Association Hall of Fame, including course designer William Diddel and golf professional Wayne Timberman.

On the former site of the J. E. Morris farm off secluded Spring Mill Road, the original Meridian Hills Country Club clubhouse began as a modest farmhouse, seen here after a fire ravaged the property. The farmhouse conversion cost in excess of $25,000. The new club facilities, designed by architect Lee Burns, were eventually remodeled to include both men's and ladies' locker rooms, an expanded kitchen area, and new restrooms, with costs capped at an additional $15,000. The original intent was to abandon the old converted farmhouse and construct a new clubhouse, one that mirrored some of the more famous country clubs in the United States, with plans heavily favoring New Jersey's Baltusrol Club. Because financing was difficult to secure, Meridian Hills Country Club continued to utilize the original, but updated facilities until a new clubhouse was finally constructed in 1950. (Meridian Hills Country Club.)

Two views of the original clubhouse, one taken from an airplane, complete with visible shadow, and one from the golf course around 1939, show the wooded beauty and unassuming character of the club. From the beginning, the conservative atmosphere of the club promoted a family-friendly atmosphere, with both gambling and alcohol forbidden. Although alcohol was eventually approved for sale in 1950, many older club members blamed prohibition for stagnation and declines in membership, as well as being responsible for the lengthy delay in funding construction of a new clubhouse. At more liberal clubs, alcohol sales were seen as a reliable and lucrative revenue stream, even stimulating dining expenditures. These additional dollars were used to assist with remodeling, upgrading facilities, and new construction projects. Regardless, prohibition allowed the club to focus on golf without the distractions of drink. (Meridian Hills Country Club.)

Meridian Hills Country Club was able to contract with William Diddel, a noted golf course architect and area resident, to design and build a championship 18-hole golf course. While the greens committee had negotiated the contract, funds were once again nonexistent. In lieu of payment, Diddel accepted a partial promissory advance toward club membership. With work commencing in the fall of 1923, modern construction equipment was also nonexistent, leaving most of the work to be completed by teams of men, horses, and stationary plows. Water lines were only directed toward tees and greens, not the fairways, but better irrigation was later added. In comparison to other Midwest courses, Meridian Hills has always ranked near the top. Pete Dye, George Fazio, and member designers have all lent modifications, but minimal course alterations remain a true testament to the skill of Diddel. As a club member for a quarter century, Diddel plays a round of golf with a very attractive caddy. (Meridian Hills Country Club.)

During the Meridian Hills Country Club's first 40 years of operation, Carl Bretzlaff served as the club's golf course superintendent. Retiring in 1965, Bretzlaff began his tenure with the club when he was hired in the spring of 1923 to remove underbrush, tame nearly 80 acres of wooded terrain, and smooth the land. Bretzlaff enjoys some infrequent downtime at the club in 1939. (Meridian Hills Country Club.)

The fruits of Bretzlaff's labor are readily apparent in this 1939 view of the course. Note the small trees and the lounging area under the shade of the tree. Considering the size of the course, both resting areas and additional tees were installed and maintained by Bretzlaff's dedicated crew. (Meridian Hills Country Club.)

Carl Bretzlaff was an esteemed member of the selective National Association of Course Superintendents, but keeping the greens green is not a solitary function. Seen here in 1938, Bretzlaff is photographed next to a vintage tractor with his arm around a mowing crew member, carrying a water can, and demonstrating the cohesiveness of his maintenance unit; Bretzlaff, even as superintendent, was a hands-on supervisor, an integral team player. Considering his 40 years of active service to the club, the loyal Bretzlaff was able to immaculately maintain the course, often under the reality of delayed pay and limited resources. The 1939 mowing crew is depicted before a workday on one of America's most noted courses. (Meridian Hills Country Club.)

Bretzlaff's equipment shop and crew ran like a well-oiled machine. A large seasonal staff and cramped work area were challenges faced by the superintendent. Despite the conditions, Bretzlaff stressed cleanliness, evident in the orderliness of the facility and workers' willingness to clean the workspace. Not one to hide behind a desk, Bretzlaff was often seen on the greens, giving advice and support to his team or engaging in physical work himself. Although the administrations of rival clubs were not always on friendly terms, Bretzlaff was known to share his wisdom and advice around Indianapolis, as well as nationally. Both photographs are from about 1939. (Meridian Hills Country Club.)

Running a country club requires more than cutting the grass, hiring a golf professional, and cooking a members' dinner. Meridian Hills Country Club was known for excellent retention of administration and support staff. Seen in a rare 1939 office appearance, Carl Bretzlaff enjoys a casual chat with the office staff. (Meridian Hills Country Club.)

Afternoons often lured 100 or more golfing members from their desks to the club. As the 1920s roared to an end and the hard times of the 1930s approached, the club offered an escape from the world's problems. Meridian Hills produced many outstanding golfers, sporting four Indiana Golf Hall of Fame members. Resident golf professionals have included Wally Sparks, Dick Nelson, and Wayne Timberman. (Meridian Hills Country Club.)

Board member and chairman of the admissions committee, Alex Holliday and his family had a keen interest in horses. Since several members voiced interest in riding, Meridian Hills Country Club became the only Indianapolis club offering horse stables and a designated bridle path around the golf course's perimeter. The stables were built near the site of the original golf cart barn, and horse boarding became an income generator. Eventually a groom and riding instructor were placed on staff. The club even purchased two horses for casual riders. Foxhunts were a unique club offering a few times a year. By 1931, the stable and horse services were contracted to a private operator, and it closed for good in 1941. This 1920s photograph shows, from left to right, Hazel Stone, Mr. Bridges, and Jane Bretzlaff enjoying the bridle path. (Meridian Hills Country Club.)

Aside from golf and horses, Meridian Hills Country Club offered many other amenities. Dining options were available from the beginning. Tennis was added in the early 1930s, while aquatics were added a little earlier. Country clubs were expected to have pools, and the competitive Indianapolis demanded no less. Public pools were a rarity across the country and nearly nonexistent in Indianapolis. Even when they were available, public pools were often considered immoral, unsafe, or unsanitary. Located directly east of the clubhouse, a 30-by-70-foot swimming pool, considered large for the times, was constructed in 1928. The club's 350 members enjoyed the pool, an appreciated oasis under the shade of maple trees, resting upon a blanket of lush green grass. The original pool was replaced in 1964 by the club's current Olympic-size model. (Meridian Hills Country Club.)

Popular even today, holiday and themed dinners and celebrations are mainstays at urban, country, and family recreational clubs. Some Indianapolis clubs have had eclectic costume dinners centered on such themes as the St. Valentine's Day massacre or the Universal Monsters. While Fourth of July events tend to be the largest and most elaborate for the club, Christmas and Easter are definite runners-up as the most popular family-fun activities. The ladies of Meridian Hills pose for the camera during a 1938 Halloween bash. The theme parties continue to this day and remain as popular breaks in the normally formal atmosphere of the clubhouse. (Meridian Hills Country Club.)

The wealthy and affluent had the means to engage in fine dining in the 1920s and 1930s. Evening dining was especially popular on Thursdays, the traditional night off for the household staff. Meridian Hills, like the other country clubs, had offered dining from the opening but suspended this service for a few years in the 1930s. The dining operations in particular were dependent on low-wage employees, and the National Recovery Act required employers to pay a minimum wage that would make the service too expensive. Rather than break the law, the directors suspended the service, eliminating the employees. This caused a rift among the members, and a number resigned, joining other clubs that still had dining service. By 1938, the service was restored; members were encouraged to return, and the rift was resolved. (Meridian Hills Country Club.)

Next to the greens crews, country clubs' kitchen staffs were the second-largest employment expenditure. The 1939 kitchen staff at Meridian Hills Country Club was unique in that the majority of the workers did not hold a minority status; however, servers were almost always African American. In comparison to other Indianapolis clubs, the staff was small, possibly due to the club's no-alcohol policy. (Meridian Hills Country Club.)

The dining facilities at Meridian Hills Country Club were comfortable and traditional, not overly fancy or lavish by country club standards. Since libations were prohibited, the club took great care in offering the finest food at reasonable prices. Through the years, the dining areas have been modified to meet the changing needs of the members. (Meridian Hills Country Club.)

Male golfers at Meridian Hills Country Club have long been accomplished competitors. Winners of Indiana state amateur tournaments include John McGuire, Henry Timbrook, and Ed Tutwiler, and multiple-title winners include John David and Dale Morey. From playing a round on the golf course, like these gentlemen pictured in the 1940s, the club has become known for supporting serious golfing competitors. (Meridian Hills Country Club.)

SEE

SAM SNEAD

The Champ of "The Masters"

18 HOLE
EXHIBITION MATCH

SAM SNEAD · DALE MOREY
JOHN DAVID · WAYNE TIMBERMAN

Meridian Hills Country Club
70th ST. & SPRING MILL ROAD

SUNDAY · MAY 30th · 2 p.m.
$2 50   CLINIC AT 1:30 P.M.

PARKING AVAILABLE

Posters were distributed throughout Indianapolis golfing venues, and the public was extended a rare opportunity to attend a club event. Masters champion Sam Snead visited Meridian Hills Country Club on May 30, 1952, for an 18-hole exhibition match with members John David, Dale Morey, and Wayne Timberman. The grounds were packed with spectators watching outstanding golfers ply their trade. (Meridian Hills Country Club.)

Early female golfers at Meridian Hills Country Club were even more successful than their male counterparts. The club hosted the U.S. Women's Amateur Championship in 1956. In the 1970s, women members brought home several more Indiana state amateur titles than the men. Women golfers, through their multiple successes, paved the way for greater acceptance of gender-integrated golf activities at the club. Given women's traditional roles at home and at country clubs, where they watched the children and played cards, conservative Meridian Hills Country Club was progressive in the roles women played at the club. From rallying support around club initiatives to decorating the new clubhouse, the ladies of Meridian Hills were recognized for contributions made to improving the club. Since family life was highly valued by the leaders of Meridian Hills and family activities were frequently visible, the club was determined to be more than just a men's club. (Meridian Hills Country Club.)

The original 1925 clubhouse had served its purpose well. The initial remodeling, along with additional refurbishments in 1946 and 1947, still was not adequate for the club. During the fall 1948 general meeting, the desire to build a new clubhouse resurfaced. Many members loved the homey quaintness of the old renovated farmhouse. After many heated discussions, 51 percent of the members voted for the plan to support a new building that could compete with other Indianapolis country clubs for years to come. Construction began immediately, and the new $230,000 clubhouse opened in August 1950. The club retained the original Meridian Hills wrought iron fire screen, placing it over a pine settle, prominently visible from the elegant entryway. The original clubhouse then served the club as a storage facility but quickly fell into ruin. Shortly thereafter, the landmark became an eyesore and was razed, much to the dismay of its occupants: owls, bats, rodents, and other pests. This 1947 photograph shows the original clubhouse, days numbered, in the stillness of winter. (Meridian Hills Country Club.)

Meridian Hills Country Club

Members of Meridian Hills Country Club had waited a long time for a new clubhouse. Some members were against the building project, while others thought the time to build was way overdue. With financing sketchy, initial plans and renderings were hung in the old clubhouse. Architect and builder Hugh Bremerman was awarded the contract to construct the new facilities. L. S. Ayres in Indianapolis, with input from the ladies of the club, provided the decorations and furnishings. The services of a landscape architect were also contracted, but Carl Bretzlaff and his staff completed the actual landscaping work. Not part of the original plans were a much needed pro shop and bathhouse, both added shortly after the August 1950 opening. (Meridian Hills Country Club).

The grand opening of the new clubhouse occurred on Sunday, August 20, 1950. Pres. William G. Davis presided over the festivities. The clubhouse accommodated 500 members, with dining capacity set at 250 diners. The kitchen was professionally designed. The south porch could be screened for use in the summer and could easily be converted for year-round use. The clubhouse opened with limited parking, but plans were in place to upgrade the amenity. The clubhouse housed the highest level of technology in its heating and cooling, plumbing, and general mechanical shop. Additional effort and expense was given to even the smallest of details, like lighting and acoustics. Much time and detail were spent on constructing a clubhouse that felt like home, yet was appropriate for hosting high-society events. For the first time in club history, a small bar was built and alcohol was available. (Meridian Hills Country Club.)

Prominent club members join grounds superintendent Carl Bretzlaff (seated) in welcoming the latest and greatest in golf cart technology to Meridian Hills Country Club. The new carts were delivered in October 1955 and considered the best available in the industry. Only the finest golf carts were worthy to travel between holes on the club's championship course. (Meridian Hills Country Club.)

Aside from emerging technologies, the 1950s brought changes to the golfing ritual. Mixed foursomes were gaining popularity and acceptance on the course. In keeping with the family atmosphere of the club, mixed foursomes were usually reserved for married couples. Prior to the 1950s, it was a rare occurrence to see couples golfing together. (Meridian Hills Country Club.)

While individual golf lessons were offered, and usually conducted by the club's golf professional, group lessons were more practical and economically feasible training forums. Group lessons empowered student members to learn and develop their strokes at their own pace, maximizing the limited availability of the club professional. Seasoned club members were recruited to provide assistance to the novices. Men and women were taught together, while children attended separate lessons. The classes were valued communal experiences that ultimately enhanced relationships and nurtured skills. On a smaller scale, the popular group-lesson format was also utilized for swimming, tennis, and even dance. (Meridian Hills Country Club.)

Keeping with the family atmosphere of the club, specific activities were regularly scheduled for families and children. There were family-friendly holiday parties, including special meet-and-greet sessions with perennial favorites Santa Claus and the Easter Bunny. The annual Fourth of July picnics were well attended and included some of the finest fireworks in the area. Swimming lessons were available and youth competitions promoted. There were doll tea parties for the young ladies and exploration days for the young gentlemen. Day camps were also offered. A playground was installed on the site of the original demolished clubhouse, and in later years, a popular teen club was initiated, as was a special dining room area for children. The club's third golf professional, Wayne Timberman, began his noted golf program, Swing Class, in which boys and girls, age 14 and under, received training and instruction on golf fundamentals. Management felt the future of country clubs rested with cultivating special memories and loyalty at early ages. (Meridian Hills Country Club.)

During the history of Meridian Hills Country Club, through both prosperous and lean years, many excellent leaders volunteered to direct and grow the club. In this historic photograph from the 1960s, several club past presidents gather for a lively evening of shared stories. The group includes Norb Shafer (1953), George VanDyke (1957), Paul Summers (1941), Bill Davis (1949), Fred Hadley (1951), Pete Wilson (1955), I. W. Sturgeon (1937), and Floyd King (1947). Membership in the club includes doctors, lawyers, and businessmen, including several business owners. Given the club's original incorporation in the city of Meridian Hills, a then-wealthy suburb of Indianapolis, the club's membership base was highly educated, wealthy, and pillars of the community. The City of Meridian Hills eventually merged into the City of Indianapolis, but the neighborhoods surrounding the club continue to be firmly nestled within the upper economic classes. Members are leaders both inside and outside the walls of the club. (Meridian Hills Country Club.)

From rolling farmland and lush forest, the Meridian Hills Country Club offers one of the finest golfing facilities in the Midwest. The rich farmland provided fertile soils for the fairways, and the luxury of more-than-adequate acreage allowed the course to display a unique and challenging character. As one of the most mature and challenging courses in Indianapolis, with some of the most interesting holes in country club golf, it is difficult to score par, but a fair course to achieve decent results. The uniqueness of the Meridian Hills course continues to earn its reputation among the most legendary courses within the community of established Indianapolis clubs. (Meridian Hills Country Club.)

The Meridian Hills Country Club of today is a vibrant and stable community. Noted for being among Indianapolis's most exclusive and expensive private clubs, the club offers value to its members. Golf facilities include the championship William Diddel–designed 18-hole course, extensive practice facilities and driving range, the Jack Barber Pro-Shop, and numerous programs and clinics for all members. For tennis, the club offers six clay courts, two hard-surface courts, and two paddle courts. Catering, dining, and banquet facilities, an Olympic swimming pool, and state-of-the-art fitness center are but a few of the additional amenities offered at Meridian Hills. The club is well poised for survival, with a steady membership base as well as a commitment to the traditions of family and a conservative management philosophy. (Meridian Hills Country Club.)

Five

THE FAMILY RECREATIONAL CLUBS

In 1933, the enterprising manager of the Broad Ripple park gathered a few friends to create a new model of a private club. His idea was to create a club environment with many of the amenities of the traditional country clubs, but more directed at family activity. His concept began with a swimming pool and tennis courts, but no golf course, and dining in a relatively formal setting, but not fine dining, and prohibition of alcoholic beverages. His club opened in the same geographic area as the traditional country clubs and appealed to much of the same clientele, remaining a haven for the affluent but more focused on the entertainment of their children.

For the following two decades, the clubs remained virtually unchanged. They were the private places of the upper class, drawing public notice only on the society pages of the local newspapers when various events were covered.

After World War II, the social order underwent a major transformation. The industrial boom created a whole new economic class of moderately wealthy families. These new families were having children at a record pace, and they required housing and entertainment facilities. They also had sufficient wealth to reach for some of the amenities that previously were reserved for the rich.

In the mid-1950s, the concept of private family recreational clubs began in earnest, with several clubs, located all around the city, opening in just a few years. These clubs all followed a design model of centering the facilities on a swimming pool and adding a space for dances, receptions, and similar activities. While a few offered dining, alcohol was generally prohibited. They were committed to a family atmosphere.

The family recreational clubs were in a way the mirror image of the country clubs. The country clubs catered to the adults and provided a few amenities for the children, while the family recreational clubs catered to the mothers and children and provided some adult activities on weekends and evenings. These clubs became the summer playgrounds of the generation known as the baby boomers.

In the 1920s, while the affluent families golfed or swam at the country clubs, for most Indianapolis residents a day at the pool meant paying a daily admission to a facility such as White City Amusement Park in Broad Ripple Village. Offering a large pool with a simulated beach atmosphere, food concessions, and perhaps a few ride attractions, these were the "clubs" of the middle class. (Indiana State Library.)

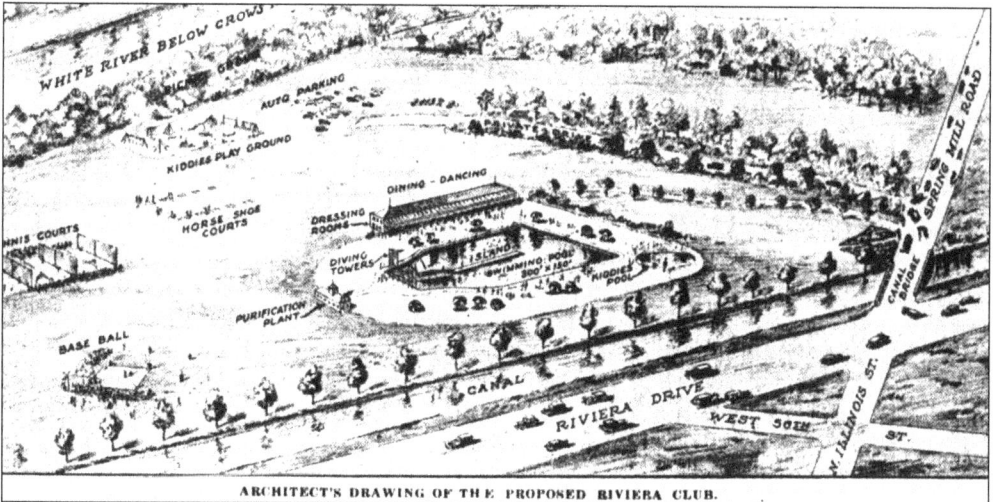

ARCHITECT'S DRAWING OF THE PROPOSED RIVIERA CLUB.

In 1932, James Mikan, an entrepreneur in the amusement park business, gathered a few friends to create a private club to offer swimming and other family-oriented entertainment to its members. He built his plan on the theory that many affluent families desired a private place for family entertainment but did not join country clubs because they offered primarily adult-oriented activities such as golf and fine dining.

Mikan and his associates were able to sell enough memberships to open the Riviera Club in the summer of 1933. Located in the same neighborhood as the country clubs, the new club appealed to the same affluent population, but with a virtually opposite offering. Riviera offered a large pool, but no golf, offered dining, but no alcoholic beverages, and offered sports activities aimed primarily at families. (Jane Bielawski.)

A typical summer day found the large pool at the Riviera Club filled with families. In the foreground, coauthor Jim Hillman's father introduces his son to swimming. Unlike the country clubs with membership in the low hundreds, Riviera attracted a membership counted by the thousands. The large member base allowed the club to expand facilities to include an indoor pool and gymnasium, while keeping the costs relatively low. (Authors' collection.)

With a pool as large as a small lake, the Riviera on a typical summer day could easily accommodate the mixed activities of a family with very young children that needed constant supervision or a group of older children enjoying the historic water slide, now a memory. (Indianapolis Times Archive/Gary Yohler.)

Riviera soon became known for its large competitive swimming program, and the indoor pool made year-round competition possible. Over the years, the club produced a remarkable number of world-class swimmers and Olympians and gained a national reputation in competitive swimming. At 75 years old, the club has weathered social and economic pressures but continues to offer family recreation to a substantial membership. (Authors' collection.)

This aerial photograph taken in 1958 shows the Riviera Club on a typical summer day. The number of cars in the parking lot illustrates the popularity of the pool. The club was originally planned for a location near the present Thirty-eighth Street and Keystone Avenue, a highly urbanized area. James Mikan was able to secure a point of land between the Central Canal (lower right) and the White River (upper left), a site that was originally used as a dump. Early news stories tell of thousands of truckloads of fill being hauled to the site to literally create the space for the club. The large outdoor pool is the dominant feature of the club grounds and remains much as originally constructed in 1933. The tennis courts have been upgraded and enlarged over the years, and the clubhouse building has been expanded to include an indoor pool and gymnasium (the high structures to the left). The facilities remain essentially the same as the club celebrates its 75th anniversary year. (Indianapolis Times Archive/Gary Yohler.)

After World War II, a group of investors took a page from the amusement park era and constructed Longacre Park on the near south side of the city. The park offered a large pool with a beachlike atmosphere, picnic areas, miniature golf, and food concessions on a daily admission basis. The park was popular among families with young children and was a busy teenage gathering place in later years. (Authors' collection.)

In the late 1950s, the owners of Longacre Park constructed a mobile home park on a large part of the land, hoping to attract residents who would become a steady source of park customers and to generate a year-round income. The pool and miniature golf course were then marketed as an amenity to the prospective residents, similar to the amenities offered in new housing additions of the time. (Longacre Park.)

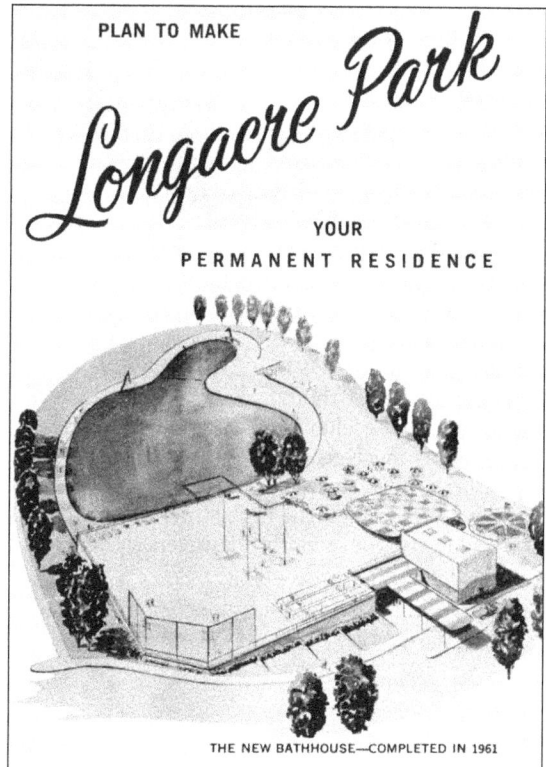

PLAN TO MAKE

Longacre Park

YOUR
PERMANENT RESIDENCE

THE NEW BATHHOUSE—COMPLETED IN 1961

On the city's west side the growing population led to the expansion of a swimming facility known as Westlake Beach. The original lake had been created by excavation for fill dirt for a railroad project and opened as a swim lake and beach in 1931. New construction in the 1950s upgraded the facility, which soon became a popular family entertainment location. (Indiana Historical Society, Bass Photograph Collection No. 24700.)

Among the popular attractions in the postwar era was miniature golf. The expansion at Westlake added a concrete and carpet course that required players to putt their way around a variety of obstacles on each hole. Like Longacre, it operated on a daily paid admission basis. In this 1958 photograph, Westlake manager Noble Trent tests his skill on the first tee. (Noble Trent.)

Attractions at Westlake Beach included a small train that ran around the property and a dance pavilion that featured a roof that could be opened for dancing under the stars. The pavilion drew popular bands and was the site of many high school proms. A drive-in theater was added, and in 1960, a concrete diving pool (seen at left below) was added to supplement the lake swimming. The addition of this filtered-water swimming pool was a major change for the facility and dramatically increased its appeal to more serious swimmers. The operation thrived until the construction of Interstate 465 around the city in the 1960s. The spreading urban growth enveloped the area, and an apartment complex now occupies the site. The drive-in theater continued for several more years but eventually closed as well. (Noble Trent.)

MIRAMAR
Club

9351 EAST WASHINGTON STREET
I N D I A N A P O L I S
C. WILBUR FOSTER & ASSOCIATES A.I.A. · ARCHITECTS

By the early 1950s, there was a growing and prosperous middle class that wanted family entertainment such as the country clubs offered but was unwilling to pay the high costs of membership. From that desire the concept of middle-class family recreational clubs developed. This new genre of clubs was tailored directly to the upper-middle-class family-entertainment market. The largest of these clubs was the Miramar Club, which opened a large pool on the east side of the city in 1955. The Miramar was designed to offer the biggest and most modern swimming and recreational facilities, with a construction budget widely reported to be $500,000. The swimming pool shown on the plans is over an acre of water and has separate pools for youngsters and toddlers, Olympic class lanes for competitive swimming, and a three-meter diving tower. The clubhouse shown on the plans would later be expanded to include an indoor pool and gymnasium. (Indianapolis Times Archive/Gary Yohler.)

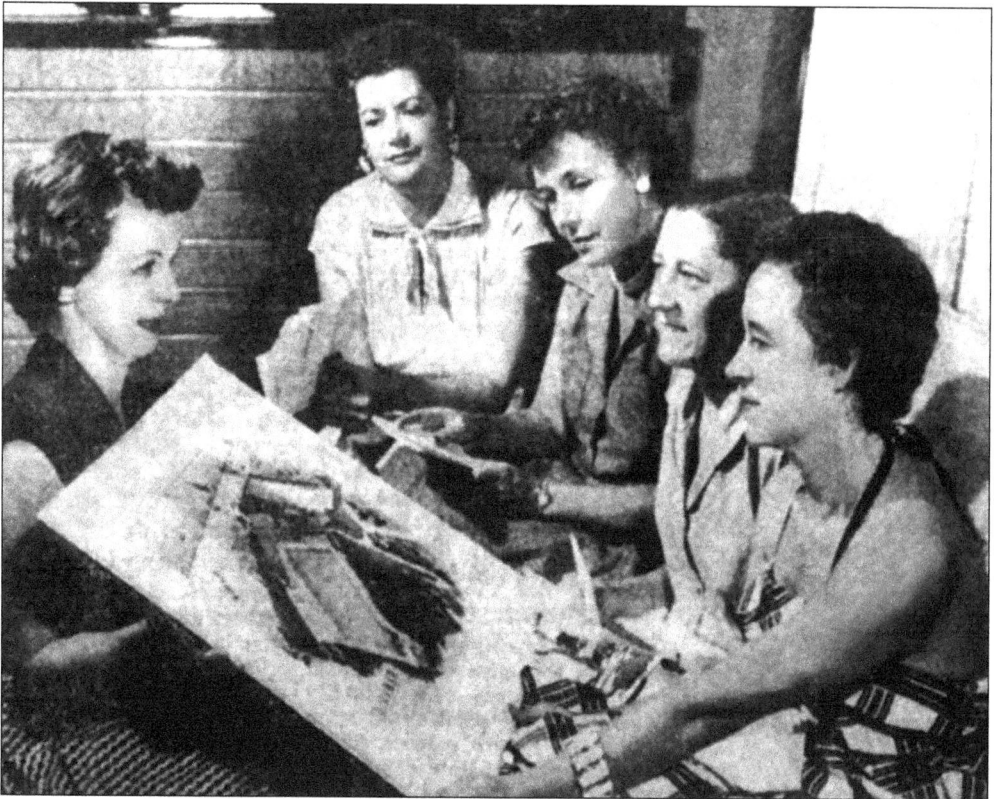

Although designed primarily as recreational facilities, the new clubs were also a social symbol for the members. The ladies were involved from the start in soliciting members and planning the activities. The Miramar ladies pictured in 1954 are gathering a charter membership of 1,000 families, with a total membership goal of 3,000 families. (Joe Young Photography.)

A few years after opening the pool facility, the Miramar Club completed the clubhouse building that included a 20,000-square-foot ballroom, lobby, and lounge. The ballroom was used for square dances, ballroom dances, and teen dances, all reserved for members and their guests. The space was also available for weddings and other events for members and their families. (Indianapolis Times Archive/Gary Yohler.)

Not being tempered by tradition as were the long-established country clubs, the new family clubs were open to innovation in programs and facilities. The Miramar Club installed a unique stainless steel indoor pool covered by an air-supported fabric dome. General manager Jack Murphy (left) is getting instructions on adjusting the air-conditioning system that also provided the air pressure to keep the building inflated. (Indianapolis Times Archive/Gary Yohler.)

Not all activity at the clubs was around the pools. Miramar general manager Jack Murphy (father of coauthor John Murphy) is seen hosting a formal reception in the ballroom at the club. Other indoor facilities included a spacious gymnasium, locker room, pool, and snack bar. Since the club did not have a dining facility, events such as weddings and banquets were catered by local services. (Joan Lekens.)

The family clubs flourished and were a popular place for teens to spend their school vacation days. The pool at Miramar was as large as a small lake and easily accommodated inner tubes and floats even on busy days. Miramar's pool was so large that for a publicity event in 1956, a water-skiing demonstration was put on using an outboard motorboat in the pool. (Jim Gilday.)

The most sought-after summer job of the 1960s and 1970s was that of lifeguard at a club pool. This was the teen dream; the pay was good, the hours were flexible, the location was the best, and the opportunity to meet girls and guys was unlimited. These Miramar lifeguards are seen next to the junior pool, a separately enclosed shallow pool for youngsters. (Jim Gilday.)

102

A common feature of the clubs was the use of large wood sundecks placed over the concrete. These decks were more inviting and were often painted in a rainbow of colors to brighten up the pool area. The decks required continual repair and replacement as the elements took a toll on the wood, and the surfaces had to be kept suitable for bare feet. (Jim Gilday.)

A typical summer afternoon at the Miramar found as many teens lounging on the decks as in the pool. A good tan was a fashion statement, and the best way to achieve it was to spend time at the club. The clubs were the places that parents felt comfortable having their teenage children spend time, feeling that they were in a safe environment with their social peers. (Jim Gilday.)

In Beech Grove, on the southeast edge of the city, the Olympia Club opened in 1956. The club featured an outdoor pool, tennis courts, and a clubhouse that provided a space for dances and parties. Designed for a membership of about 1,000 families, the facilities were similar to Miramar but smaller in scale. (Beech Grove Public Library.)

The Olympia pool was a summer haven for the young families in Beech Grove. The club offered a place for the children to take swimming lessons, become involved in a swim team, or just play in the water on a summer day. In an age of stay-home mothers, the club was the place for the mothers to socialize while the youngsters were in the pool. (Beech Grove Public Library.)

Using a design common for the day, the Olympia pool accommodated regulation competition swimming lanes in the main section and provided a deep diving area offset to one side. The design provided the flexibility of a large general swimming area for regular use and easy transformation to a competition arrangement by simply installing ropes and floats to mark the lanes. The offset diving well provided a space with sufficient depth to allow use of a three-meter diving board, while keeping the diving activity clear of the general swimmers in the pool. Below, the Jackson children enjoy another common feature, a shallow wading pool separate from the main pool. Some of the similarity in design may be attributed to the fact that local architect C. Wilbur Foster designed several of the clubs. (Above, Beech Grove Public Library; below, Margie Jackson.)

The 1950s was a growth period for the family clubs comparable to the growth of the country clubs in the 1920s. On the north side of the city the Dolphin Club and Devon Country Club appeared, and in the town of Speedway on the west side of the city the Speedway Recreational Club (later renamed Westwood Country Club) was established. While each club strived to be different, the postcard views above and below show a pool design that could be any of several clubs. The competition lanes, separate diving pool, separate wading pools, and wood decks were uniformly popular appointments of the family clubs. In the case of Speedway Recreational Club, they were able to capitalize on the terrain of the property to create a unique two-level clubhouse that offered a terrace overlooking the pool. (Frank Tout.)

On the north side of the city, the founders of the Westchester Estates residential development created a recreational area in the community intended to be used as a private club for the homeowners. The fact that the plan allowed the homeowners to be members but did not require membership nearly caused an early death for the club. Homeowners without children, or not interested, did not join the club. This caused a shortfall in the membership required for operation of the club at a reasonable per member cost. A decision was made to open the membership, and sufficient interest was developed in nearby neighborhoods to keep the club viable. By 1966, Westchester Estates Recreational Club had a stable and active membership and fielded its first swim team, pictured below. (Jane Bielawski.)

While their counterparts at the country clubs played in golf tournaments, the family clubs engaged in swim meets with the other area clubs. These events were highly organized, staffed by volunteer parents, and grew to the point that many clubs had paid coaches for their swim teams. Pictured is a meet between Westchester Estates Recreational Club and the Azionaqua Swim Club of Zionsville in 1969. (Jane Bielawski.)

Swim team activities were among the most popular organized activities at the clubs. Parents formed swim team support groups that provided transportation to events at other clubs; acted as officials at meets; outfitted their teams in specially designed shirts, jackets, and swimsuits; and conducted award ceremonies at the end of each season. Pictured here is the 1975 awards night at Westchester Estates Recreational Club. (Jane Bielawski.)

Holiday weekends were a busy time at the clubs, especially Memorial Day, marking the opening of the season, and Labor Day, which signaled the end of the season. Westchester annually celebrates the Labor Day weekend with an all-club cookout and picnic, a time for family gathering and play, and a last chance for the youngsters to enjoy the summer break from school. (Jane Bielawski.)

While the adults were doing the cooking and preparing the picnic, the youngsters were at play in the pool. Although the pools at most public parks did not allow the use of floats and inner tubes, Westchester and many other clubs did, much to the delight of the younger set. (Jane Bielawski.)

At the far northeast corner of the city, the Northeastway Club was another example of a club created to serve as an amenity for a housing development. The club organized a swim team and was quite competitive for several years in the 1960s. The facility was eventually taken over by the city and is now a part of Sahm Park. (Devon Country Club.)

Most of the family clubs were outdoor-only venues, but many of the swimmers who began at these clubs soon became members of the Indianapolis Athletic Club, Riviera, or Miramar to be able to swim in the indoor pool all winter. A remarkable number of the swimmers who began at the family clubs went on to be successful at college and national levels. (Devon Country Club.)

Six

THE LITTLE POOL CLUB THAT COULD

Off Millersville Road in central northeast Indianapolis, the Devon Country Club is nestled down an unpretentious wooded drive marked by a solitary sign. A short drive through an open metal gate reveals tennis courts, a parking area, a retro-cool arched art deco pavilion (designed by Bruce "Bebe" Atkinson), a large open lowland field caressing the scenic banks of Fall Creek, a block bathhouse and deck, and of course, the pool.

They were believers. Under the guidance and vision of club founder Albert Diebold, a dedicated crew of dreamers canvassed the neighborhoods surrounding the land that was to become Devon. As a result of diligent, often door-to-door recruitment, Devon opened in 1956 with the support of 500 families; another 50 or so families were placed on a waiting list. The club promoted affordable, quality family recreation in a beautiful outdoor setting, an easy sell to the then upscale and postwar-prosperous area residents.

From stellar beginnings, the Devon Country Club had some early concerns. The main amenity, the swimming pool, suffered a collapsed wall shortly after construction, falling victim to persistent flooding and active groundwater. The original pool was replaced in 1958 with an aboveground model, decorated by ornate and colorful perimeter tiles. In addition, the club planned a future nine-hole golf course, a component that never materialized.

Aside from the addition of two tennis courts to complement the original three playing surfaces, new pool decking, and modern pavilion, the maintenance and upkeep of the club have preserved the facility almost as it appeared in the early years.

Devon continues its tradition of competitive swimming and tennis. The club remains under family leadership, with many of the founding families still active. Considering the economics and virtual demise of family recreational clubs in Indianapolis, Devon is a true survivor. The future of Devon Country Club will build upon the traditions of the past, with the promise of continuing fun and new family memories.

The Dolphin Club is gone. The Olympia Club is gone. Many great Indianapolis swimming pools live only in memories—Longacre, Lakeshore, Miramar, Westlake, and so many other casualties. Devon Country Club is a survivor. "Reminiscent of the lazy summer days of the 1950s, Devon Country Club offers families something unique—a relaxed environment with a variety of adult and child activities that promise a lifetime of great memories," is the promise in the club's promotional materials. Experiences that were once common in Indianapolis now are considered unique. Aside from the Riviera Club, different in design, development, and intent, Devon shares the spotlight with Westchester Estates Recreational Club as one of the two remaining examples of traditional family recreational clubs in Indianapolis. Family picnics, like this family enjoying a cookout at Devon on Labor Day 1970, remain a common sight on the grounds of Devon today. (Devon Country Club.)

The entryway to Devon Country Club is easy to miss. Prior to houses being built to the north, and a small sign stuck in the ground to alert visitors, the unmarked access road remained obscured by woods on both sides. Traveling a short distance, a simple metal gate permits entry to the parking lot on the eastern boundaries of the property, front and forward of the facilities, the tennis courts are visible directly ahead, with the clubhouse and swimming pool set off to the north. This picture from 1969 was taken from the parking area and shows two members discussing the day's festivities. Middle-class cars were seen in the lot, typically not upscale sedans common in the country clubs. Regardless of postwar prosperity, and what was considered upscale housing at the time, the club catered to families in the immediate area, and not the pretensions of the affluent. The club simply existed to provide quality family summer outdoor entertainment. (Devon Country Club.)

Far from the aquatic diversions offered in summer, these photographs of the Devon pool in winter show the original block clubhouse and state-of-the-art filtering and chemical facility. Shortly after 1956 organizational efforts by Albert Diebold and other believers, the club opened with a pool, warm-weather clubhouse, and three tennis courts. The original inground pool collapsed due to excessive groundwater pressure, and in 1958, an aboveground model was built as a replacement. The new pool was noted for its colorful perimeter pool tiles, one of the few excesses the club management approved. Since Devon was built for summer activities only, several club off-season events were held at such varied locations as the Columbia Club, Riverside Amusement Park, and the naval armory. Bowling teams and member house parties proved popular during the winter months. (Devon Country Club.)

Contrasting winter and summer photographs show the deepwater diving area at the club. High platform boards are a rarity at modern swimming facilities due to high insurance costs. Devon maintains both high and low dive equipment. Many of the family recreational clubs of the era had similar diving areas or separate diving tanks, as was the case with the Riviera Club; the Riviera built an independent, partially aboveground pool with spectator windows available for underwater viewings. Through the years, Devon made diving lessons available to members, and several members were successful divers both inside and outside the club. (Devon Country Club.)

Swimming excellence has always been a trademark of Devon Country Club. These pictures show the 1969 Devon swim team and starting swim meet lineup. In the team photograph, club members may spot Marc Diebold, son of original organizer Albert Diebold and owner of a noted Indianapolis marketing business. The Fourth of July and Labor Day holiday weekends were always active at the club, including cookouts and aquatic activities and competitions. Original swim team parents were active in the development of new swimmers, and many Devon swimmers have received college scholarships for their swimming skills. To this day, Devon successfully competes with several area clubs in the Indianapolis Community Swim Conference, continuing the swim team tradition for second- and third-generation 6 to 17 year olds. (Devon Country Club.)

To have one of the most competitive swim teams in Indianapolis, scheduled swim practices continued to be a summer staple of club activity. Pictured here is the 1969 Devon Swim Team preparing to warm up for a meet, several members testing the water temperature with their toes, just moments away from an exhilarating 45-minute practice. Devon's pool is now heated. Keeping with the importance of Devon's competitive swim efforts, Devon champion Julie McArch is pictured with a first-place ribbon and her 1969 club trophy. Devon takes pride in its individual swimmers and celebrates accomplishments with club recognition. (Devon Country Club.)

In the top picture, two Devon swimmers, Carol and Jennie, are all smiles holding a 1969 club trophy. Trophies and ribbons are coveted, but plentiful bounties, as this picture of Devon's 1970 swim team demonstrates. One of the keys to Devon's success and longevity is its commitment to family. There are many third-generation swimmers at the club. The club started with 500 enthusiastic families, with 50 more families on the waiting list. Even with intense competition for leisure time, Devon has been able, in lean years, to maintain club membership of at least 300 families. (Devon Country Club.)

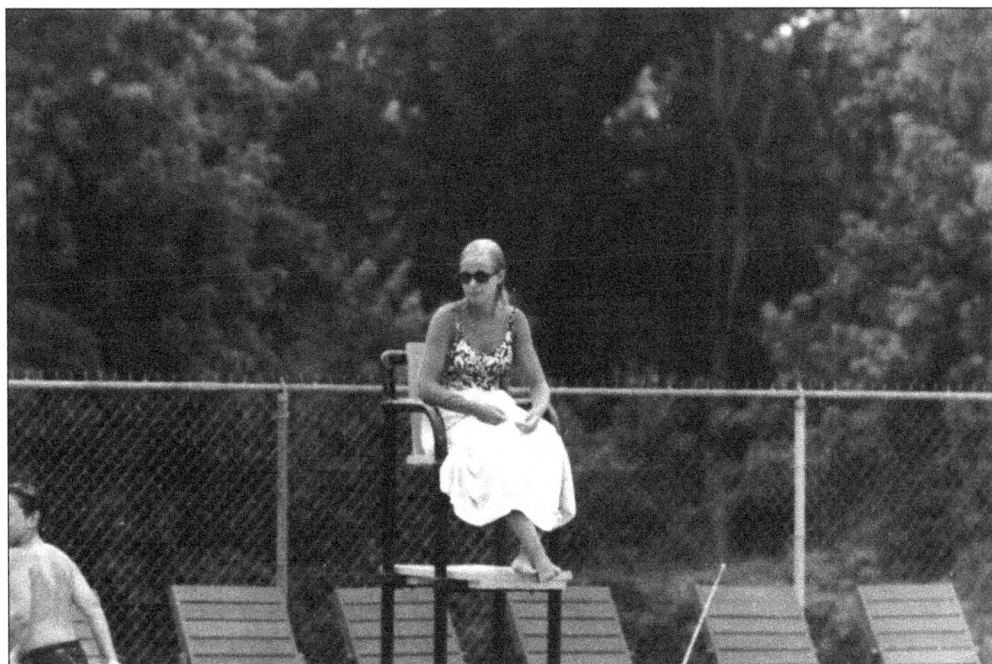

The pool was not just reserved for competitions. Seen here is "miss safety," lifeguard Terry, on careful watch over Devon swimmers. Lifeguards, as well as all staff and board members, preferred being addressed by their first name. Whether taking a dip in the pool or lounging on the deck or ever-present picnic tables, summer at Devon meant warm sun and cool water. The tree line behind the pool rises from the banks of Fall Creek. Immediately in back and to the right of the pool is an open field. Not much has physically changed at the club in over half a century. A distinctive curved, wooden arch pavilion, built adjacent to the clubhouse by Bruce "Bebe" Atkinson, drain tiles around the tennis courts, and a wooden pool deck were added under the guidance of Kip Barnes's leadership. (Devon Country Club.)

Although there is much emphasis on swimming at Devon, both competitive and recreational, tennis has also played an important part in club history. These 1970 photographs show both cornerstone activities at Devon. The 1960s and 1970s were flourishing times for tennis at the club. Sponsored by 7-Up, Devon players took ball and racket through national-level competitions. Club member Frank Kearney earned men's singles championships several years running. Continuing the tradition of competitive tennis today, Devon's tennis team is a member of the United States Tennis Association. Ensuring future success, Devon continues to provide group and individual tennis lessons, as well as conduct novice and family tennis activities. (Devon Country Club.)

Tennis spectators watch the annual Calcutta Labor Day Tennis Tournament and competitive action on the courts. Note the beverage cans on the table and chair. Devon has always allowed food and beverage, including alcohol by those over the age of 21, to be brought onto the premises by members. Initially the Devon tennis program was rooted on the skills of a dozen committed players, but with growing popularity, the club added two more courts during the presidency of Mike Glenn. While the tennis courts were originally coated black with white lines, since tennis balls were only produced in white, 1968 saw the introduction of newly coated red and green playing surfaces. With new drain tiles around the courts, a Labor Day tennis tournament is underway. (Devon Country Club.)

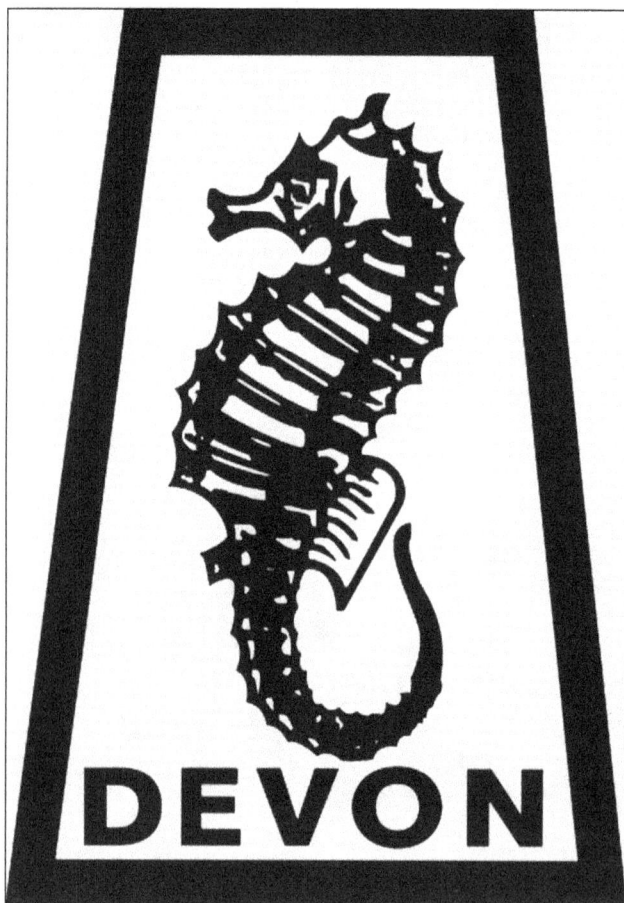

The Devon Board of Directors and club manager were photographed in February 1970. While the directors will not be taking a swim in the pool, they probably would be quite proud of the little pool club on the northeast side of Indianapolis, still located on Millersville Road a short distance from Forty-sixth Street. From social events like fashion shows, hayrides, and bingo nights, to the mini-triathlons, which began in the 1980s, and themed pool parties with extravagant decorations, Devon remains the little club that can. Pictured is the original and current friendly sea horse mascot on the Devon Country Club logo. (Devon Country Club.)

Seven

THE NEW REALITY

The social clubs of Indianapolis give a window through which one can view the changes in the social, cultural, and economic climate of the city. Each type of club has risen to prominence and then declined, some to remain active but dramatically altered—others to fade away altogether.

The causes of these changes are as varied as the interests that sparked the birth of the clubs themselves. The ethnic groups that were only a generation away from the old country have now largely assimilated into the society as a whole, the wealthy who once had large homes near downtown have relocated to suburban estates, the middle-class mothers are now working and have little time to spend at the pool with the children, the civil rights movement challenged the clubs' ability to be exclusive, good restaurants abound, and improved public golf courses compete with the private clubs. In addition, the general tone of society has become less formal, and interest in joining social organizations of any sort has diminished.

Many of the clubs were able to navigate these turbulent waters and make adjustments that enable them to continue to be viable. The all-male city clubs opened their membership to women. The country and family recreational clubs eliminated racial and ethnic barriers to membership. Gone are the days when a "Gentiles Only" sign guarded the gates at the Riviera Club.

Among the city clubs, the Columbia Club and the Propylaeum have been able to adapt their operations and remain active parts of the social scene. The Athenaeum now houses a YMCA, theater, and restaurant, and the Indianapolis Athletic Club has become residential condominiums. The country clubs have reduced costly offerings and developed more family programming. Most of the family recreational clubs have simply faded away. Highway construction negatively impacted Longacre Park and Westlake Beach.

The future of the remaining clubs is uncertain. Club managers and members express a consensus that the general trend to smaller and fewer private clubs is likely to continue. The options include consolidation and mergers, conversion to semiprivate or public facilities, or simply closure.

The Miramar Club, largest of the middle-class family clubs, was established on 25 acres of what was in 1954 a rural spot far east of the city. The club flourished from 1954 until the mid-1970s, finally closing in 1978. Designed to accommodate a membership of 3,000 families, it offered a swimming pool larger than a football field, a unique stainless steel indoor pool housed in an inflated dome, a ballroom, a gymnasium, tennis, and a golf driving range. In the early years, the club was beyond the city bus lines, so there was a private bus that traveled a route through the neighborhoods such as Irvington to take the youngsters to and from the club. But suburban growth soon enveloped the property, membership gradually declined, and the property became too valuable for other uses to continue as a recreational club. The site is now one of a series of shopping centers along heavily traveled Washington Street. (Authors' collection.)

On the west side, in the town of Speedway, the Speedway Recreational Club was opened in 1956 and renamed the Westwood Country Club a few years later. Located on a rolling, mostly wooded 26-acre parcel on High School Road, the club continued operation until 2004. Plans for redevelopment of the property are unknown, but restoration to recreational club use is unlikely. (Authors' collection.)

The Dolphin Club opened in 1959 on a 23-acre parcel on Guion Road. The club offered swimming, a large picnic and sports area, and a clubhouse with a ballroom. The club operated for about 20 years but gradually experienced a decline in membership. The YWCA acquired the property. A change in the primary mission of the YWCA and the operational and maintenance costs resulted in closure in 2004. (Authors' collection.)

Like the Jackson children enjoying the waters at the Olympia Club, many spent their youth in these magical places. No one could foresee that their club would become a park or shopping center or that an interstate highway around the city would literally obliterate two of the most favored teen hangouts. A bit like old sailors who seek to recapture a moment of the good times at sea, club members often find their ship at the salvage yard awaiting its final voyage to oblivion. But sometimes, they can close their eyes and remember a gentler time. (Above, Margie Jackson; below, authors' collection.)

INDEX

Visit us at
arcadiapublishing.com

·····································

www.ingramcontent.com/pod-product-compliance
Lightning Source LLC
Chambersburg PA
CBHW050637110426
42813CB00007B/1837